DYMOND'S CAPITAL TRANSFER TAX

SECOND EDITION

FIRST SUPPLEMENT

BY

ROY R. GREENFIELD, LL.B. (Lond.)

Formerly Deputy Controller of the Capital Taxes Office

Oyez Longman

OYEZ LONGMAN PUBLISHING LIMITED
21-27 LAMB'S CONDUIT STREET
LONDON WC1N 3NJ

ISBN 0 85120 824 X

Second Edition 1983
First Supplement 1984

Dramrite Printers Limited, London, England

CONTENTS

PREFACE

Since the publication of the Second Edition at the end of 1982 there has been no reform of Capital Transfer Tax comparable with the Finance Act 1982. The Finance Bill of March 1983 contained ten clauses relating to the tax, but they were all lost because of the general election. The Finance (No 2) Act 1983 restored six of them, comprising new tables of rates, the abolition of the £250,000 exemption limit for gifts to charities, an increase from 20 per cent to 30 per cent in the relief for tenanted agricultural property and minority shareholdings in unquoted companies, an increase from eight to ten years in the period for instalments of tax, the abolition of the deemed domicile rule for the Channel Islands and Isle of Man, and the extension to England and Wales and Northern Ireland of the Scottish principle that tax on real (or heritable) property is a testamentary expense unless the testator directs otherwise. The remaining four clauses are to be reintroduced next year and are printed near the end of this Supplement (*see* p 58).

Three cases have been decided in the Court of Appeal. *Inglewood* v *IRC* and *Egerton* v *IRC* were both concerned with accumulation and maintenance trusts, and *IRC* v *Trustees of Sir John Aird's Settlement (No 1)* related to the notorious Newspaper-Franco device. The *Aird* case is of particular interest because of a long judgment by Oliver LJ discussing the interpretation of statutes. Other cases dealt with in this Supplement are *Finch* v *IRC* in the Chancery Division, *Willett* v *IRC* before the Lands Tribunal, and *Bond* v *Pickford*, a Capital Gains Tax case in the Court of Appeal.

The Government has indicated that it intends to consolidate the law of Capital Transfer Tax, and Sched 9 to the Finance Act 1983 included five relevant pre-consolidation amendments, none of them amounting to much. It is a little surprising that the Revenue did not take the opportunity of amending para 4(7) of Sched 5 to the Finance Act 1975 to bring it into line with s 22(4) of that Act and so make clear that divorcees may qualify for the 'surviving spouse' relief even if their interests terminate in lifetime: *see* p **1094** of the Second Edition.

The five Double Taxation Conventions made since 1975 (with the Republic of Ireland, South Africa, the United States, the Netherlands and Sweden) were all based on the OECD Draft Convention of 1966. A new (1982) OECD Model Double Taxation Convention on Estates and Inheritances and on Gifts was published in 1983 and may affect not only the negotiation of future conventions but also the interpretation of those already made. A concise description of the new Model is therefore given in this Supplement (*see* p 24).

In July 1983 the Treasury issued a revised version of their booklet *Capital Taxation and the National Heritage*. The law on this subject is unchanged, but there have been some modifications of official practice, and the chapter on National Heritage Property has been updated accordingly.

I acknowledge with gratitude the help received from Adrian Tytherleigh, of the Capital Taxes Office in London, and from Kathleen Patrick, of the Capital Taxes Office in Edinburgh. But, like the main volume, this Supplement has no official authority and the views expressed are solely those of the author.

In this book, as in the statutes, the word 'tax' means Capital Transfer Tax unless the context otherwise requires. References to pages of Volume 1 of the Second Edition are shown in bold type.

The Supplement states the law and practice as at 30 September 1983.

11 October 1983 RRG

TABLE OF CASES

TABLE OF STATUTES

Page references in **bold** type indicate that the text has been reproduced.

TABLE OF STATUTORY INSTRUMENTS

Page references in **bold** type indicate that the text has been reproduced.

OECD MODEL CONVENTIONS

Page references in **bold** type indicate that the text has been reproduced.

CONVENTIONS AND DOUBLE TAXATION AGREEMENTS BETWEEN THE UNITED KINGDOM AND OTHER COUNTRIES

PART 1: TEXT

Introduction (pp 1-8)

The Finance (No 2) Act 1983 has made the following changes, all with effect from 15 March 1983:

(1) the £55,000 threshold mentioned on p **1** is now £60,000;

(2) the limit of £250,000 for the charity exemption (p **2**) is abolished;

(3) the 20 per cent agricultural relief and the 20 per cent business relief (p **4**) are increased to 30 per cent;

(4) persons who have acquired a domicile in the Channel Islands or the Isle of Man (p **5**) are no longer treated as retaining their United Kingdom domicile indefinitely;

(5) the eight-year period for instalments (p **6**) is increased to ten years.

In addition, the rates of interest on unpaid tax and on repayments, which were previously 9 per cent for transfers on death and 12 per cent for other transfers (p **6**), have been reduced by SI 1982 No 1585 to 6 per cent and 8 per cent respectively with effect from 1 December 1982.

Interpretation and Construction of the Taxing Acts (pp 10-44)

STRICT CONSTRUCTION

Lord Reid's observations in *Luke* v *IRC* [1963] AC 557, cited at p **14**, were relied on by the Revenue in *IRC* v *Trustees of Sir John Aird's Settlement (No 1)* [1983] STC 700 as establishing a general principle of construction. The Court of Appeal did not object to that but could not accept that para 6(7) of Sched 5 to the Finance Act 1975 showed an 'obvious intention' on the part of the legislature. Oliver LJ referred to *Lumsden* v *IRC* [1914] AC 877 (mentioned at p **17**), where Viscount Haldane said at p 892:

> 'But a mere conjecture that Parliament entertained a purpose which, however natural, has not been embodied in the words it has used if they be literally interpreted is no sufficient reason for departing from the literal interpretation.'

Oliver LJ also quoted Lord Reid's remarks in *Stenhouse Holdings Ltd* v *IRC* (1970), 46 TC at p 682 (cited at p **17**) as indicating a broader approach to construction than was previously regarded as permissible, and said:

> 'Nevertheless there are limits within which it is permissible to reframe the express words which the legislature has chosen to use. Where it is clear that a literal reading produces a wholly unreasonable or administratively impossible result and there is a context for adopting a more restricted reading, there is no particular difficulty. *Camille Dreyfus* v *IRC* [1956] AC 39 and *IRC* v *Plummer* [1980] AC 896 were both cases in which a more limited construction was deducible from other provisions of the statute which pointed to the legislature's intention. Nor is there any particular difficulty where (as, for instance, in *R* v *Federal Steam Navigation Co* [1947] 1 WLR 505) it is impossible, on a literal construction, to give any intelligible meaning at all to the particular provision. But this case does not fall under either of these heads. Construed literally the paragraph is perfectly intelligible and perfectly capable of operation. The problem is simply that the consequences go a great deal further than the legislature can rationally have been supposed to have foreseen. That, no doubt, points to a more limited meaning having been intended, but one must, I think, start from the position that the intention has to be deduced from the words which Parliament has chosen to use and that they must be fairly capable of the more limited construction sought to be put upon them. If not, they must be applied as they stand, however strongly it may be suspected that this was not the real intention of Parliament.'

Jones v *Wroxham Park Estates Ltd* [1980] AC 74 was another case in which the literal interpretation of the words used produced consequences which could hardly have been foreseen. Lord Diplock at p 105 said:

> 'I am not reluctant to adopt a purposive construction where to apply the literal meaning of the legislative language used would lead to results which clearly defeat the purpose of the Act. But in doing so the task on which a court of justice is engaged remains one of construction, even where this involves reading into the Act words which are not expressly included in it. *Kammins Ballrooms Co Ltd* v *Zenith Investments (Torquay) Ltd* [1971] AC 850 provides an instance of this; but in that case the three conditions that must be fulfilled in order to justify this course were satisfied.
>
> (1) First, it was possible to determine from a consideration of the provisions of the Act read as a whole precisely what the mischief was that it was the purpose of the Act to remedy;

(2) secondly, it was apparent that the draftsman and Parliament had by inadvertence overlooked, and so omitted to deal with, an eventuality required to be dealt with if the purpose of the Act was to be achieved; and

(3) thirdly, it was possible to state with certainty what were the additional words that would have been inserted by the draftsman and approved by Parliament had their attention been drawn to the omission before the Bill passed into law.

Unless this third condition is fulfilled, any attempt by a court of justice to repair the omission in the Act cannot be justified as an exercise of its jurisdiction to determine what is the meaning of a written law which Parliament has passed. Such an attempt crosses the boundary between construction and legislation.'

In the *Aird (No 1)* case, cited above, Oliver LJ said that neither the first nor the third of the conditions stated by Lord Diplock could be said with confidence to be satisfied, and he was unable to find any justification as a matter of construction for departing from the literal meaning of the words. For further details of the judgment, *see* p 38, *infra*.

PUNCTUATION

The relevance of punctuation, side-notes and cross-headings in statutes (pp 18–19) was considered also in *R* v *Schildkamp* [1971] AC 1, where Lord Reid said at p 10:

> '. . . it may be more realistic to accept the Act as printed as being the product of the whole legislative process, and to give due weight to everything found in the printed Act . . . I would not object to taking all these matters into account, provided that we realise that they cannot have equal weight with the words of the Act. Punctuation can be of some assistance in construction.'

In the same case Lord Upjohn said at p 28:

> 'When the court construing the statute is reading it through to understand it, it must read the cross-headings as well as the body of the statute, and that will always be a useful pointer as to the intention of Parliament in enacting the immediately following sections . . . A side-note is a very brief precis of the section and therefore forms a most unsure guide to the construction of the enacting section, but it is as much a part of

the Bill as a cross-heading and I can conceive of cases where very rarely it might throw some light on the intentions of Parliament just as a punctuation mark.'

In *Hanlon* v *The Law Society* [1981] AC 124, Lord Lowry said at p 198:

'I consider that not to take account of punctuation disregards the reality that literate people, such as Parliamentary draftsmen, punctuate what they write, if not identically, at least in accordance with grammatical principles. Why should not other literate people, such as judges, look at the punctuation in order to interpret the meaning of the legislation as accepted by Parliament?'

R v *Governor of Brixton Prison, ex parte Naranjan Singh* [1962] 1 QB 211 and *Luby* v *Newcastle-under-Lyme Corporation* [1965] 1 QB 214 are sometimes cited as examples of the irrelevance of punctuation even in modern statutes. In the first case the court construed a statute as if a comma were inserted; in the other the Court of Appeal treated a comma as if it were not there. But that does not mean that they disregarded the punctuation. They looked at it and decided that the intention of the legislature, as manifested by the words used, must prevail over the punctuation.

In *Marshall* v *Cottingham* [1982] Ch 82 Megarry V-C said: 'I accept, of course, that the day is long past when the courts would pay no heed to punctuation in an Act of Parliament.'

The latest case on the subject appears to be *Egerton* v *IRC* [1983] STC 531, noted at p 42, *infra*. The point to which the Court of Appeal attached most importance was that the last part of s 71(2) of the Finance Act 1978 was separated from the first part only by a semi-colon. In the first part Parliament had made clear its intention that the section as a whole was to be construed and applied on the footing that it came into force on 11 April 1978. Correspondingly, in the judgment of the Court, it had made clear its intention that the wording of the last part of the subsection should be read and applied on the same footing.

It appears that brackets, like other punctuation marks, are disregarded in statutes before 1850: *Devonshire (Duke of)* v *O'Connor* (1890) 24 QBD 468, *per* Lord Esher MR at p 478; *R* v *Speyer* [1916] 1 KB 595 *per* Lord Reading CJ at p 614. In modern statutes brackets may be important. For example, in *Carver* v *Duncan* [1983] STC 310 Vinelott J said at p 339: 'The use of parentheses is at least an indication that the words in parentheses were intended as subordinate to — a qualification or gloss on — the preceding words which in themselves are the primary definition.'

THE WORD 'DEEMED'

It was an exaggeration to say at p **26** that the term 'deemed' is not used in the Capital Transfer Tax provisions. Certainly it does not have the importance that it once had for Estate Duty, and the draftsman of Part III of the Finance Act 1975 seems to have scrupulously avoided it; but the word is used in the Finance Act 1976 — *see*, eg, ss 97, 105(1), 107(5) and 108(2) — and in subsequent legislation. A topical example is s 71(2) of the Finance Act 1978, which begins by providing that the section shall be deemed to have come into force on 11 April 1978. In *Egerton* v *IRC* [1983] STC 531 the taxpayers argued that a reference later in s 71(2) to the coming into force of the section must refer to the date of Royal Assent, but the Court of Appeal decided against them for the reasons explained at p 42, *infra*.

Similarly, in *Sanderson* v *IRC* [1956] AC 491, where the phrase was 'where for the purposes of estate duty there pass', the House of Lords held that this included gifted shares which were 'deemed to pass'.

Interest on Estate Duty (p 70)

The rate of interest has been reduced from 9 per cent to 6 per cent with effect from 1 December 1982 (SI 1982 No 1584).

Excluded Property (pp 103–107)

The paragraph at p **106** relating to 'Islanders' is now obsolete. Under s 12 of the Finance (No 2) Act 1983, s 45(1)(*c*) of the Finance Act 1975 ceases to have effect in relation to transfers of value made, or other events occurring, on or after 15 March 1983. Section 49 of the Finance Act 1977 has been repealed. The rule about Islanders' savings — para (iii) (*b*) at p **103** — is not affected.

Free Estate (pp 122–129)

Damages for loss of expectation of life (*see* foot of p **124**) have been abolished by s 1(1) of the Administration of Justice Act 1982. Section 4(2) of that Act provides that the damages recoverable for the benefit of the estate shall not include 'any damages for loss of income in respect of any period after that person's death'. These provisions apply to deaths on or after 1 January 1983.

The result is that where a person dies instantaneously in an accident, the damages recoverable under the Law Reform (Miscellaneous Provisions) Act 1934 are normally limited to funeral expenses. Where the death is not instantaneous there may be a possibility of damages in respect of pain and suffering, including any suffering caused by the injured person's awareness that his expectation of life has been shortened.

Property Subject to a Contract (pp 129–130)

It was suggested at p **129** that para 5 of Sched 10 to the Finance Act 1975 applies to transfers on death in much the same way as s 3 of the Finance Act 1894. This is not now thought to be correct. The settlement made by the widow in *Re Harmsworth* [1967] Ch 826 was an exercise of her power to dispose of the property, not an exclusion or restriction of it, and para 5 would not be in point (cf p **1131**). As explained at p **1000**, property comprised in a settlement made for full consideration is not for that reason exempt from Capital Transfer Tax unless it comes within para 1(2) (*c*) of Sched 5 to the 1975 Act.

Initial Meaning of 'Transfer of Value' (pp 139–142)

It might have been mentioned here that, where a person gives consideration for an interest in possession in settled property, any question whether the giving of consideration is a transfer of value must be determined without regard to para 3(1) of Sched 5 to the Finance Act 1975: *see* s 69(7) of the Finance Act 1978. The operation of this rule is explained at pp **1086–1087**.

Intention of Gratuitous Benefit, etc (pp 143–156)

The meaning of 'shares or debentures not quoted on a recognised stock exchange' is discussed at p **151**. Securities dealt in on the Unlisted Securities Market are not regarded as quoted for this purpose: *see* Statement of Practice 18/80 printed at p 497 of Vol 2.

What is said above in relation to *Re Harmsworth* applies equally to *Re Bateman* [1925] 2 KB 429, cited at p **154**. It is now thought that para 5 of Sched 10 to the Finance Act 1975 would not be relevant to a transaction of the *Bateman* type.

Free or Cheap Loans (pp 186–193)

The first paragraph on p **193** needs amendment as a result of s 9 of the Finance (No 2) Act 1983, under which the exemption for gifts to charities made on or after 15 March 1983 is not limited to £250,000 or any other figure (*see* p 20, *infra*). The paragraph should now begin thus:

> 'Under s 117(5) loans to political parties within one year of death are not subject to the £100,000 limit in para 11 of Sched 6 to the 1975 Act. For the purposes of that paragraph and paras 10, 12 and 13 of Sched 6 (gifts to charities, for national purposes and for the public benefit) . . .'

Dispositions for Maintenance of Family (pp 207–215)

Paragraph 5 of Sched 9 to the Finance Act 1983 (a pre-consolidation amendment) inserts a reference to s 46(5) of the Finance Act 1975 (*see* p **213**) into para 4(10) of Sched 5 to the last-mentioned Act. The result is that references in s 46(5) to any property or to an interest in any property include references to part of any property or interest. It is understood that the Capital Taxes Office had already been interpreting s 46(5) in that way.

Alteration of Dispositions taking effect on Death (pp 215–235)

There is a misprint in the new version of s 47(1A) on p **226**. After the words 'settled by his will' there should be added 'and, within the period of two years after his death'.

Employee Trusts (pp 363–368)

The limit of £1,250 a year mentioned in line 12 on p **365** has been increased by s 25 of the Finance Act 1983 to 'the relevant amount', meaning not less than £1,250 and not more than £5,000 but (subject to that) 10 per cent of the participant's salary.

The Cumulation Principle (pp 405–408)

Paragraph 3 of Sched 9 to the Finance Act 1983 makes a small pre-consolidation amendment to s 37(1)(*b*) of the Finance Act 1975. In its original form, s 37(1)(*b*) provided that to work out the rate of tax you had to aggregate the value of a chargeable transfer with the values previously transferred by chargeable transfers made by the same transferor. The resultant figure was usually known as the transferor's cumulative total. Section 93 of the Finance Act 1981 excluded gifts more than ten years old from the cumulative total, but the word 'previously' disappeared, so that on a literal construction the latest chargeable transfer might have had to be included twice. It is scarcely thinkable that the Revenue would have adopted that construction, or that any court would have supported them if they had, but para 3 of Sched 9 makes the point quite clear.

The reference in para 3 to 'previous chargeable transfers' does not mean that simultaneous chargeable transfers are not aggregated with each other. As stated at pp **420–421**, this is covered by s 43(3) of the 1975 Act, under which two or more chargeable transfers by the same person on the same day are taxed at the same rate as a single transfer of the same total value. Section 43(3) is subject to an exception where s 43(2) applies, in which case one or more transfers are treated as being previous to the other(s).

Indexation of Rate Bands (p 409)

Under s 8(1) of the Finance (No 2) Act 1983 indexation is not to apply to chargeable transfers in the year beginning 6 April 1983. Instead, s 8(2) provides new scales of rates rather more generous than those which would have been available under s 91 of the Finance Act 1982. Paragraphs 2 to 7 of Sched 15 to the Finance Act 1980, summarised at pp **408–409**, apply to these new scales.

Rates on Death and within Three Years of Death (pp 410–413)

Section 8(2) of the Finance (No 2) Act 1983 substitutes new tables in s 37(3) of the Finance Act 1975 with respect to chargeable transfers made on or after 15 March 1983. The new scale of rates on death is as follows.

Table 1—Rates on Death after 14 March 1983

Slice of chargeable transfers which *exceeds*	*and does not exceed*	*Cumulative tax at minimum of range – ie, figure in col 1*	*Rate of tax on slice within the range*
£	£	£	per cent
60,000	80,000	nil	30
80,000	110,000	6,000	35
110,000	140,000	16,500	40
140,000	175,000	28,500	45
175,000	220,000	44,250	50
220,000	270,000	66,750	55
270,000	700,000	94,250	60
700,000	1,325,000	352,250	65
1,325,000	2,650,000	758,500	70
2,650,000	–	1,686,000	75

Lifetime Rates (pp 417-419)

The new scale of lifetime rates under s 8(2) of the Finance (No 2) Act 1983 is as follows.

Table 2—Lifetime Rates after 14 March 1983

Slice of chargeable transfers which *exceeds*	*and does not exceed*	*Cumulative tax at minimum of range – ie, figure in col 1*	*Rate of tax on slice within the range*
£	£	£	per cent
60,000	80,000	nil	15
80,000	110,000	3,000	17½
110,000	140,000	8,250	20
140,000	175,000	14,250	22½
175,000	220,000	22,125	25
220,000	270,000	33,375	30
270,000	700,000	48,375	35
700,000	1,325,000	198,875	40
1,325,000	2,650,000	448,875	45
2,650,000	—	1,045,125	50

Transfers Reported Late (pp 422–427)

The Finance Bill of March 1983 proposed to repeal s 114(8) of the Finance Act 1976 (mentioned at p **427**) with effect from 1 April 1983. Evidently the intention was to rely on the Finance Act 1975, Sched 4, para 23, as amended by clause 71 of the Bill, which is discussed at p 19, *infra*. Clause 71 was lost because of the general election, but the Chancellor of the Exchequer has announced that he will reintroduce it in 1984 and that it will take effect from 1 April 1983. It is printed at p 59, *infra*.

Valuation of Unquoted Shares and Debentures (pp 447–477)

The figure of 20 per cent in the last paragraph on p **448** became 30 per cent with effect from 15 March 1983, as explained at p **12**, *infra*.

Valuation of Freehold and Leasehold Property (pp 486–492)

In *Willett* v *IRC* (1982), 264 EG 257, the Lands Tribunal had to value a tenanted farm for Capital Transfer Tax on a death in May 1977. The tenant declined to give his age but was thought to be 66 or 67. There was a possibility that he might surrender his tenancy in return for money, but at the date of valuation negotiations for a surrender had been unsuccessful. The taxpayer's valuer took the tenant's expectation of life as 11.39 years and discounted the vacant-possession value for 12½ years on the assumption that vacant possession would not be obtained until a year or more after the tenant's death. The Tribunal agreed with the Revenue valuer that the tenant would probably retire in his lifetime and that the vacant-possession value (estimated at £66,000) could reasonably be discounted for eight years. After adding the value of the rent for those eight years, the resultant figure was increased by about 10 per cent to reflect the value to the sitting tenant. The value so determined was £39,000, as against £28,000 estimated by the taxpayer and £45,000 by the District Valuer.

The Lands Tribunal remarked that in valuing property under s 38 of the Finance Act 1975 it is right to assume that it is suitably lotted (*see Ellesmere* v *IRC* [1918] 2 KB 735) — a point which neither valuer had taken directly into account. In fact the tenant was persuaded to surrender his tenancy and the property was sold in four lots to two buyers for a total of £126,750, but that was 17 months after the death and prices had risen.

Tax Deposit Certificates (p 493)

A new prospectus (Series 6) for Certificates of Tax Deposit was introduced with effect from 11 October 1982. The main differences from the old series are that—

(1) the rates of interest earned will be realigned with current rates on each anniversary of the deposit, rather than on the second and fourth anniversaries only;

(2) the rates of interest may vary according to the size of the deposit. It is expected that deposits of £100,000 or over (which must be remitted direct to the Bank of England) will earn higher rates.

'Value Transferred' (pp 503-509)

Because of s 8 of the Finance (No 2) Act 1983 the grossing table on p **508** applies only to lifetime transfers between 9 March 1982 and 14 March 1983. A grossing table for later transfers is given below.

Table 3 — Grossing table for lifetime transfers after 14 March 1983

Net £	*Multiplier*	*Gross* £
60,000	20/17	60,000
77,000	40/33	80,000
101,750	5/4	110,000
125,750	40/31	140,000
152,875	4/3	175,000
186,625	10/7	220,000
221,625	20/13	270,000
501,125	5/3	700,000
876,125	20/11	1,325,000
1,604,875	2	2,650,000

Scottish Agricultural Leases (pp 521-523)

Section 98 of the Finance Act 1981 and s 97 of the Finance Act 1982 apply only to tenancies held by an individual or held jointly by individuals, and not to tenancies held by a partnership or a company. Joint occupation under a joint tenancy is not in Scots law the same thing as a tenancy held by a partnership: cf *Haddo*

House Estate Trustees v *Davidson* [1982] SLT (Land Court) 14, a case on notice to quit.

Reduction in Value of Agricultural Property (pp 523–542)

The 20 per cent relief for tenanted land in para (*b*) on p **525** was increased to 30 per cent by s 10(2) of the Finance (No 2) Act 1983. The increase has effect in relation to transfers of value made, and other events occurring, on or after 15 March 1983.

Reduction in Value of Business Property (pp 542–558)

MINORITY SHAREHOLDINGS IN UNQUOTED COMPANIES

The 20 per cent relief in para (3) on p **544** was increased to 30 per cent by s 10(1) of the Finance (No 2) Act 1983 in relation to transfers of value made, and other events occurring, on or after 15 March 1983. The reference to 20 per cent on p **542** applies only to transfers and events before that date.

SETTLED PROPERTY USED BY A LIFE TENANT

It is noted at p **547** that before 10 March 1981 settled property could not qualify for the 30 per cent relief (under para 3(1) (*c*) of Sched 10 to the Finance Act 1976) if used for the purposes of a business carried on solely by the life tenant. That statement remains unchallenged, notwithstanding the anomaly that relief *was* available if the life tenant carried on the business in partnership. However, in *Finch* v *IRC* [1983] STC 157 a claim was made for business relief (30 per cent at the date of death, but now 50 per cent) under para 3(1)(*a*).

The facts were as follows. The deceased was tenant for life of an estate of 5,500 acres, of which 1,845 were in hand. A claim for agricultural relief in respect of 1,000 acres of the land in hand was agreed. 446 of the remaining 845 acres were woodland subject to relief under Sched 9 to the Finance Act 1975. Of the balance of 399 acres, 142 were occupied by the deceased for less than two years before his death. The claim for business relief was limited to the remaining 257 acres.

The notional transfer of value which took place on the death in September 1977 included the business of farming and forestry carried on by the deceased. The value attributable to that business had to be reduced by 30 per cent under paras 2(1) and 3(1) (*a*) of Sched 10 to the 1976 Act. At first sight the value attributable to the business could not include any of the settled land, which was not in fact part of the business. But the trustees relied on para 6 of Sched 10, which says that the value of a business is its net value under para 14(2) of Sched 4 to the 1975 Act. Paragraph 14(2) says that the net value of a business is the value of the assets used in the business (including goodwill) reduced by the amount of any liabilities incurred for the purposes of the business.

On a literal interpretation of paras 6 and 14(2) the trustees might appear to be entitled to relief. Vinelott J, however, held that the phrase 'assets used in the business' could not be construed in isolation. It was part of a provision for ascertaining 'the net value of a business'. The meaning of that last phrase would be perfectly well understood if it stood alone. The net assets of a business are the balance of the assets after deducting the liabilities. In striking a balance only those assets which could be said to be assets of the business would be brought in. Paragraph 14(2) should not be read as giving the phrase 'the net value of a business' an artificial meaning wholly divorced from its ordinary meaning.

In the opinion of the learned judge, the purpose of para 14(2) was to refine and clarify the way in which the balance of net assets was to be ascertained. The words 'assets used in the business' should be construed as meaning 'assets of the business which are used in the business'. So construed, the provision would exclude assets which appeared in the balance sheet but were not in fact used in the business. It would also exclude settled land occupied by a tenant for life and used by him in his business.

If para 14(2) were construed as the trustees contended, there would be an overlap between sub-paras (*a*) and (*c*) of para 3(1). The interest of a deceased partner in the assets of a partnership would include land owned by him and used by the partnership (though not in the ordinary sense an asset of the partnership) and the land itself would attract relief under para 3(1)(*c*). The existence of this overlap, the judge said, afforded an indication that para 3(1) (*a*) was not intended to extend to such land.

The language of para 14(2) construed as a whole, said Vinelott J, was not fairly capable of bearing the meaning which the trustees sought to extract from it. Even if it were capable of bearing that meaning it would be 'fairly and equally open' to more than one construction. It would therefore be permissible to look at subsequent legislation to resolve the doubt: *Kirkness* v *John Hudson & Co Ltd* [1955] AC 696, 710–713. Schedule 10 to the 1976 Act has been amended by the Finance Act 1981, s 100, which by inserting a new sub-para (*d*) into para 3(1) specifically gives relief to land which immediately before the transfer was used wholly or mainly for the purposes of a business carried on by the transferor and was settled property in which he was then beneficially entitled to an interest in possession.

So the trustees failed in their attempt to make s 100 in effect retrospective. It was clearly not intended to be retrospective, because it is expressed to relate to transfers made on or after 10 March 1981.

The case is likely to come before the Court of Appeal early in 1984. One might suppose that it is not of topical interest because (1) the limit of 1,000 acres for agricultural relief was abolished by the Finance Act 1981, and (2) if the property does not qualify for agricultural relief, business relief is available under s 100 of that Act as explained above. The important point, however, is that if the appeal succeeds such property may qualify for business relief at 50 per cent under para 3(1) (*a*) instead of (or as well as?) relief at 30 per cent under para 3(1) (*d*).

VALUATION

Paragraph 6 of Sched 10 to the Finance Act 1976 is explained at p **551**. Its meaning was further considered in *Finch* v *IRC, supra.*

Exceptions from Liability (p 586)

The references in para (3) to 'charity' and '£250,000' do not apply to gifts made after 14 March 1983: Finance (No 2) Act 1983, s 9, discussed at p 20, *infra.*

Certificates of Discharge (pp 592–593)

The last paragraph on p **593** seems to be wrong and should be deleted. If the deceased's taxable estate is increased by an order of court under the Inheritance (Provision for Family and Dependants) Act 1975, para (ii) on that page meets the situation. The 'taxable estate' includes property in which the deceased had an interest in possession under a settlement. It makes no difference that the order of court increased the value of the deceased's free estate and not that of the settled property. Trustees of settlements should therefore be wary in cases in which the Inheritance Act may apply, bearing in mind the court's discretion to extend the time limit in s 4 of that Act (*see* p **238**).

Incidence of Tax (pp 595–626)

FREE REAL ESTATE

The rule in para (4) on p **600** has been abrogated by s 13(1) of the Finance (No 2) Act 1983, with the result that testamentary expenses now include Capital Transfer Tax on free real estate in the United Kingdom unless the will shows a contrary intention. Section 13(1) substitutes for s 28(1) of the Finance Act 1975 a new s 28(1) and (1A), which reads as follows:

'(1) Where personal representatives are liable for tax on the value transferred by a chargeable transfer made on death, the tax shall be treated as part of the general testamentary and administration expenses of the estate, but only so far as it is attributable to the value of property in the United Kingdom which—

(*a*) vests in the deceased's personal representatives, and

(*b*) was not, immediately before the death, comprised in a settlement.

The provision made by this subsection shall have effect subject to any contrary intention shown by the deceased in his will.

(1A) Where any amount of tax paid by personal representatives on the value transferred by a chargeable transfer made on death does not fall to be borne as part of the general testamentary and administration expenses of the estate, that amount shall, where occasion requires, be repaid to them by the person in whom the property to the value of which the tax is attributable is vested.'

Paragraph 8(*b*) of Pt II of Sched 1 to the Administration of Estates Act 1925, mentioned in the fourth line of p **601**, has been repealed (along with the corresponding Northern Irish provision) by Pt II of Sched 2 to the Finance (No 2) Act 1983 with effect from 26 July 1983.

It had already been decided in *Re Dougal* [1981] STC 514, cited at p **601**, that heritable property in Scotland should not bear its own tax unless the will so directed. The new s 28(1) extends the *Dougal* principle to real property in England, Wales and Northern Ireland. It is understood that this legislation was discussed in advance with The Law Society and other professional bodies, and there is reason to expect that it will be generally welcome. The following points are worthy of note:

(1) Under s 13(3) the new rule applies only to deaths on or after 26 July 1983. In relation to earlier deaths, as explained at pp **601–602**, opinion is divided on whether the *Dougal* principle would be adopted by an English court. In practice, by extra-statutory concession, the Capital Taxes Office in England has given executors the option of following or not following *Dougal* and paying tax accordingly.
(2) The new rule applies only to property in the United Kingdom. Free property outside the United Kingdom, whether movable or immovable, must continue to bear its own tax unless the will directs otherwise. This is understood to be so even in Scotland, though on the face of it the reasoning of *Dougal* would seem capable of extending to a specific bequest of foreign property. Where legacies are payable out of a mixed fund of British and foreign property they must, in the absence of a contrary intention, bear their due proportion of the tax on the foreign property (*see* p **605**).
(3) The new rule has no application to settled property over which the deceased exercised a general power of appointment by will — para (1) at p **600**.
(4) Real property in the United Kingdom appears to be the only exception to the rule that property subject to the Inland Revenue charge bears its own tax unless the will directs otherwise.
(5) For the meaning of 'any contrary intention shown by the deceased in his will' *see* pp **614–617**. As noted at p **615**, it has been held to be not enough that the will contains a direction to pay testamentary expenses out of particular property or charges the property with such expenses. There must also be an intention to exonerate some other class of property from the liability; but the court will usually infer an intention to exonerate unless the property is undisposed of by the will or passes under some other title. Thus a direction charging real property with its own tax is arguably ineffective if there is undisposed-of personalty out of which the tax can be paid.
(6) The new s 28(1A) in effect restates the old s 28(1) as interpreted in *Dougal*.
(7) Statement of Practice E17, noted at p **601** and printed at p 494 of Vol 2, is superseded.

TAX ON FOREIGN PROPERTY

The citation of *Re Sebba, Lloyds Bank Ltd* v *Hutson* at p **617** should have been [1959] Ch 166 or [1958] 3 WLR 605.

ADJUSTING THE BURDEN OF TAX

The original s 28(1) of the Finance Act 1975, mentioned in the last paragraph on p **624**, has been replaced by a new s 28(1) and (1A) quoted in full above under the heading of 'Free Real Estate'. Section 28(1A) still uses the words 'where occasion requires'. The meaning of this phrase, as interpreted in *Christie's Trustees* v *Christie's Trustees* [1943] SC 97, is explained at pp **624-625**; but that case was distinguished in *Re Dougal, supra*. It is thought that what is said at pp **624-625** is still correct, subject to deletion of the word 'personal' in the first line of p **625**.

The statement at p **625** that the s 28(4) charge does not include the costs of settling the tax is plainly wrong, in view of the last sentence on p **626**. Section 28(8) of the Finance Act 1975, which is the authority for that sentence, has been amended by s 13(2) of the Finance (No 2) Act 1983 with effect from 26 July 1983. It now says: 'References in this section (except subs (2)) to tax include references to interest on tax and, in subss (3) to (5), to costs properly incurred in respect of tax.' One may therefore assume that the references to tax in subss (1), (1A) and (2) do *not* include the costs of paying it. The new s 28(8) is not restricted to *deaths* after 25 July 1983, because s 13(3) refers also to other events on which tax is chargeable after that date.

Accounts (pp 628-634)

The words 'relevant property' in para 2(2A) of Sched 4 to the Finance Act 1975 have been replaced by the words 'appropriate property': Finance Act 1983, Sched 9, para 4. This avoids any possible confusion with 'relevant property' as defined by s 102 of the Finance Act 1982 for the purposes of the discretionary trust regime. The word 'relevant' in line 13 of p **630** should now be 'appropriate'.

Where the death is on or after 1 April 1983, the gross value of £25,000 in para (*b*) on p **631** is increased to £40,000 and the £1,000 in para (*d*) is increased to £2,000 by the Capital Transfer Tax (Delivery of Accounts) (No 3) Regulations 1983 (SI 1983 No 1039) and the Capital Transfer Tax (Delivery of Accounts) (Scotland) (No 2) Regulations 1983 (SI 1983 No 1040). These regulations relate to England and Wales and Scotland and came into operation on 1 September 1983. The regulations for Northern Ireland (SI 1981 No 1441, printed at pp 395-396 of Vol 2) remain unamended for the time being, but the position is under review.

In England and Wales, with effect from 1 September 1983, a new flat-rate probate fee of £80 has replaced the *ad valorem* scale for estates between £25,000 and £40,000 net. As a general rule, where an estate is subject to a flat-rate fee no account will be due, and *vice versa*. But this is not always so. For instance, an estate might be below the £40,000 limit but not an 'excepted estate' because it contained settled property. An account would be required even though a flat-rate probate fee would be charged.

In Scotland no new confirmation fee structure is proposed to accompany the new 'excepted estate' limit. No changes are being made in the rules governing applications for confirmation to an estate. The inventory must therefore continue to be completed and presented to the Sheriff Clerk in the normal way.

Inspection for Valuation (p 636)

Under the Criminal Justice Act 1982, ss 37, 38(1), (6) and (8), 46(1) and (4) (*a*) and 75, the £20 fine in para 11(2) of Sched 4 to the Finance Act 1975 has become (except in Northern Ireland) a fine not exceeding level 1 on the standard scale (currently £25).

Instalments (pp 638–643)

In relation to chargeable transfers on or after 15 March 1983, the provisions for payment of tax by eight yearly or sixteen half-yearly instalments (in paras 13, 14 and 15 of Sched 4 to the Finance Act 1975) are replaced by provisions for payment by ten equal yearly instalments: Finance (No 2) Act 1983, s 11(1). This fits in with the ten-yearly charge on discretionary trusts (p **1137**). Where the instalment option is available, one instalment is payable in each year of the period between one ten-year anniversary and the next.

With effect from 15 March 1983 also, s 11(2) increases to £20,000 the figure of £5,000 in para 13(3) of Sched 4 — *see* para (5) at pp **638** and **641**. This seems fair, in view of inflation since 1975 and the 30 per cent discount given by s 10 of the same 1983 Act — *see* p 12, *supra*.

Interest on Tax (pp 643–645)

With effect from 1 December 1982 the rate of interest on unpaid tax (and on repayments of tax) is 6 per cent if the chargeable transfer was made on death and 8 per cent in other cases: SI 1982 No 1585. In view of para 19(2) of Sched 4 to the Finance Act 1975, the lower rate applies also to the extra tax payable on death when a transferor dies within three years of the transfer.

Acceptance of Property in Satisfaction of Tax (pp 645-649)

A new edition of the Treasury booklet *Capital Taxation and the National Heritage* was published in July 1983 at a price of £2.50. Appendices B and C to the 1980 booklet (mentioned at p **646**) are Appendices A and B to the 1983 booklet, and Chapter 14 of the 1980 booklet (p **647**) is Chapter 12 of the 1983 booklet. The first sentence on p **648** should now be: '(iii) Is the object of especial importance for the study of some particular form of art, learning or history?'

As stated at p **648**, ss 50 and 51 of the Finance Act 1946 were repealed by the National Heritage Act 1980. The reference to them in s 78(4) (*b*) of the Finance Act 1976 has now been deleted by para 6 of Sched 9 to the Finance Act 1983.

Corrections (pp 650-652)

Paragraph 23(3) of Sched 4 to the Finance Act 1975 (p **651**) provides that, in any case of fraud, wilful default or neglect by a person liable for tax, proceedings for recovery can be brought at any time within six years after the fraud, default or neglect comes to the knowledge of the Board. Clause 71 of the Finance Bill of March 1983 (which was lost because of the general election) proposed to extend this provision to cover fraud, wilful default or neglect by a settlor where tax is chargeable under the discretionary trust regime. The Chancellor of the Exchequer announced in July 1983 that clause 71 would be reintroduced in 1984 with effect from 1 April 1983. It is printed at p 59, *infra*.

The new clause will apply, for example, where the settlor failed to disclose chargeable transfers, so that the trust's cumulative total (*see* p **1143**) appeared to be less than it actually was.

Appeals to the Special Commissioners (pp 658-659)

It will usually simplify and shorten the hearing before the Special Commissioners if the facts can be agreed beforehand (*see* pp 503-504 of Vol 2). However, the parties need to be very careful when agreeing a statement of facts, because it will be binding on them; they cannot go behind it and contend that the facts were otherwise: *Symons* v *Weeks and others* [1983] STC 195.

Transfers between Husband and Wife (pp 665–672)

As noted at p **667**, the limit of the exemption for spouses domiciled overseas kept pace with the tax threshold of £15,000, £25,000, £50,000 or £55,000 between 27 March 1974 and 14 March 1983. It remains at £55,000 notwithstanding the increase of the threshold to £60,000 in the Finance (No 2) Act 1983.

Gifts to Charities (pp 672–676)

The limit of £250,000 in para (*b*) on p **672** has been removed by s 9(1) of the Finance (No 2) Act 1983 with effect from 15 March 1983. The result is that all gifts to charities are exempt, even though made on death, unless they come within the exceptions at pp **682–687**.

Gifts to Political Parties (pp 676–678)

The eight political parties in the list on p **677** qualified for exemption as a result of the general election in June 1983, and so did the Social Democratic Party. Three other parties (all Irish) each got one seat in the House of Commons but failed to get the necessary 150,000 votes.

Gifts for National Purposes, etc (pp 678–680)

To the list of heritage bodies on p **678** there should now be added the Historic Buildings and Monuments Commission for England (Finance Act 1983, s 46).

Gifts for the Public Benefit (pp 680–682)

Paragraph (*e*) at p **681** is strictly interpreted. Where property is given as a source of income for the upkeep of other qualifying property, only the income can be used. If a source of capital is required, the answer is to set up a maintenance fund (*see* pp **822–834**).

Application for the exemption should be made in the first instance to the Capital Taxes Office, not the Treasury. If the body concerned has not been previously approved, the applicant should submit all relevant documents, such as trust deeds and (if the body is incorporated) its memorandum and articles of association, with full details of its assets, expected income and forecast expenditure.

Partial Exemption (pp 687-711)

The £250,000 limit for gifts to charities mentioned at pp **687** and **691** has (as noted above) been removed with effect from 15 March 1983.

In consequence of s 8 of the Finance (No 2) Act 1983, Table 4C at p **695** applies only to deaths between 9 March 1982 and 14 March 1983. A table for later deaths is given below.

Table 4D — Grossing table for deaths after 14 March 1983

Net	Fraction	Gross
£		£
60,000	10/7	60,000
74,000	20/13	80,000
93,500	5/3	110,000
111,500	20/11	140,000
130,750	2	175,000
153,250	20/9	220,000
175,750	5/2	270,000
347,750	20/7	700,000
566,500	10/3	1,325,000
964,000	4	2,650,000

In connection with Examples 2, 5, 7, 9, 10, 13 and 14 at pp **692-706** it should be remembered that in Scotland a specific bequest of heritable property does not bear its own tax unless the testator so directs: *Re Dougal* [1981] STC 514. In England, on deaths before 26 July 1983, the Capital Taxes Office gives executors the option of following *Dougal* in relation to real property and paying tax accordingly. The rule in *Dougal* has been made statutory for later deaths (*see* pp 15-17, *supra*).

Death on Active Service, etc (pp 743-746)

Because of changes in military law the list of Women's Services in para 1(3) of Sched 7 to the Finance Act 1975 is no longer needed for the purposes of the exemption. Paragraph 1(3) and the relevant words in para 1(2) have been repealed by the Armed Forces Act 1981, Sched 5.

National Heritage Property (pp 799-834)

As noted above with reference to pp **645-649**, a new edition of the Treasury booklet *Capital Taxation and the National Heritage* mentioned at p **799** was published in July 1983. The reference at p **801** to Chapter 7 of the booklet relates to Chapter 6 of the new edition, which incidentally explains that trees and underwood may share in the exemption if they contribute to the scenic or scientific interest of the land on which they stand. The definition of 'historically associated object' at the foot of p **801** (para 8.4 of the old booklet) has been modified, and there is now no reference to 'a considerable period (usually many generations)'. According to para 7.4 of the new edition the object must have a close association with a particular building and make a significant contribution, whether individually or as part of a group or scheme of decoration, to the appreciation of that building or its history.

Where an object is lent to a public collection for special exhibitions, para 5.7 of the booklet says that the duration of the loan need not exceed six months in any two-year period (as stated at p **804**) or such longer loan and period as would be reasonable in appropriate cases, except that the duration need not exceed 25 per cent of the period. The paragraph also gives examples of what is meant by 'exhibitions which are properly organised and meet adequate security standards'.

Private treaty sales to heritage bodies (pp **807–808**) are free not only from Capital Transfer Tax but also from Capital Gains Tax, and this is taken into account when calculating the 25 per cent 'douceur' (as illustrated in Appendix A to the Treasury booklet). Such sales are also relieved from Value Added Tax.

MAINTENANCE FUNDS

Paragraphs 10.7 to 10.13 of the old booklet, mentioned at p **824**, are replaced by paras 9.7 to 9.14. In the old para 10.11 the Treasury said that the trustees could not use the fund to finance new buildings or to acquire fresh land, but the new para 9.12 accepts that the purchase of additional farm land to generate a higher income for the fund may qualify as an improvement. Improvements should be undertaken only after making proper provision for the maintenance of the heritage property.

The accounts to be furnished to the Treasury (p **825**) should include an adequate record of any accumulations of income made during the life of the fund.

Exempt Government Securities (pp 836–841)

Clause 68(2) of the Finance Bill published in March 1983 proposed to insert a new sub-para (2AA) after para 3(2A) of

Sched 7 to the Finance Act 1975. Under this, para 3(2A) was not to apply where a reversionary interest in property expectant on the termination of a qualifying interest in possession subsisting under the first settlement was settled on the trusts of the second settlement before 10 December 1981. Clause 68 was lost because of the general election, but the Chancellor of the Exchequer has announced that it will be reintroduced in 1984 and will take effect from 15 March 1983. It is printed at pp 58–59, *infra*.

Clause 68(2) will do the same for para 3(2A) as clause 68(1) will do for s 121(1) of the Finance Act 1982 (*see* p 36, *infra*). It will not be retrospective to 9 March 1982 because in some rare cases the taxpayer may be better off if the property is treated as remaining in the first settlement.

Islanders' Savings (p 842)

It should be noted that National Savings Income Bonds are *not* excluded property within para 5 of Sched 7 to the Finance Act 1975.

Visiting Forces (pp 842–843)

With effect from 1 January 1983 the words 'citizen of the United Kingdom and colonies' on p **842** are replaced by 'British citizen, British Dependent Territories citizen or British Overseas citizen': British Nationality Act 1981, s 51(3). A brief summary of that Act is given at pp **947–948**.

'Islanders' (pp 850–853)

Section 45(1)(*c*) of the Finance Act 1975 has ceased to have effect in relation to transfers of value made, and other events occurring, on or after 15 March 1983: Finance (No 2) Act 1983, s 12. Section 49 of the Finance Act 1977 has been repealed by Pt II of Sched 2 to the 1983 Act. Consequently, the text at pp **850–853** applies only to transfers of value and other events before 15 March 1983.

Situs of British Government Securities (p 857)

National Savings Income Bonds are securities registered on the National Savings Stock Register and are situate in the United Kingdom.

Domicile and Residence (pp 869-884)

As indicated above, s 45(1)(*c*) of the Finance Act 1975 has been repealed with effect from 15 March 1983. Paragraph (*c*) at the top of p **870** is therefore obsolescent. So also are:

(1) para (*c*) on p **879**;
(2) the references to limb (*c*) of s 45(1) on pp **879-884**;
(3) the reference in para (6) on p **880** to s 49(1) of the Finance Act 1977, which has now been repealed.

The result is that the Channel Islands and the Isle of Man are treated as foreign countries for the purposes of Capital Transfer Tax, except that they enjoy privileges in respect of agricultural property (pp **523-542**) and national savings (p **842**).

Double Taxation Relief (pp 889-994)

THE OECD MODEL CONVENTION

The OECD Draft Double Taxation Convention on Estates and Inheritances, referred to at p **896** and later pages as the 1966 Model Convention, has been replaced by the 1982 Model Double Taxation Convention on Estates and Inheritances and on Gifts. As the name indicates, the main new feature is that taxes on gifts *inter vivos* are now included within the scope of the Convention.

The new Model does not have any direct effect on Capital Transfer Tax, but indirectly it may affect it in two ways:—

(*a*) future double taxation conventions entered into by the United Kingdom will probably conform more closely to the new Model than past conventions have done;
(*b*) the new Model (and the commentaries on its articles) may affect the interpretation of existing conventions. The introductory report by the OECD Committee on Fiscal Affairs contains the following passage:

'The Committee on Fiscal Affairs has examined the problem of conflicts of interpretation which could arise as a result of changes in the text of the Articles or of the Commentaries. The Committee considers that existing conventions should, as far as possible, be interpreted in the spirit of the new Commentaries, even though the provisions of existing conventions do not yet contain the more precise wording of the 1982 Estate Tax Model. Member countries wishing to clarify their positions in this respect may do so by means of an exchange of letters between competent authorities in accordance with the mutual agreement procedure. Even in the absence of such an exchange of letters, these authorities would use the mutual agreement procedure to secure this interpretation in particular cases.'

It is therefore thought that a concise explanation of the new Model may be of interest to readers of *Dymond*. Its text is printed at pp 64-75, *infra*.

Chapter I: Scope

Article 1 says that the Convention shall apply (*a*) to estates and inheritances where the deceased was domiciled, at the time of his death, in one or both of the Contracting States, and (*b*) to gifts where the donor was domiciled, at the time of the gift, in one or both of the States.

This is broadly equivalent to Article 1 of the Convention with the Netherlands (p **960**), except that there is no mention of settlements. Our conventions with other countries are not expressly limited by reference to the domicile of the deceased or the donor.

Article 2 deals with the taxes covered and has four paragraphs, the first of which applies the Convention to taxes on estates and inheritances and on gifts imposed by a Contracting State or its political subdivisions or local authorities. There are, of course, no such local taxes in the United Kingdom; and, as noted at p **939**, the Convention with the United States does not extend to taxes levied by individual American states.

The second paragraph of Article 2 says that taxes on estates and inheritances include taxes imposed by reason of death in the form of taxes on the *corpus* of the estate, of taxes on inheritances, of transfer duties, or of taxes on *donationes mortis causa*; and taxes on gifts include taxes imposed on transfers *inter vivos* only because such transfers are made for no, or less than full, consideration. Thus, for example, Capital Gains Tax charged on a gift of property would not be covered, because that tax would be imposed just the same if the property had been sold.

The third paragraph lists all the taxes covered by the Convention when it is signed. The fourth paragraph extends it to any identical or substantially similar taxes which are imposed afterwards, and also requires the competent authorities to notify each other, at the end of each year, of changes which have been made in their respective taxation laws.

None of the conventions made by the United Kingdom contains anything resembling the first and second paragraphs of Article 2. The Double Taxation Agreement with India (which is not a member of the OECD) includes only the third paragraph. Other conventions made by the United Kingdom include the third and fourth paragraphs, except that the obligation to notify changes is found only in the conventions with the United States and the Netherlands and omits the words 'at the end of each year'.

Chapter II: Definitions

Paragraph 1 of Article 3 provides for only two definitions. The first says that, unless the context otherwise requires, the term 'property which forms part of the estate of, or of a gift made by, a person domiciled in a Contracting State' includes any property the devolution or transfer of which, under the law of a Contracting State, is liable to a tax covered by the Convention. This is a new definition, which has no counterpart in the 1966 Draft. It is not found in any United Kingdom conventions, for the simple reason that they do not use the term quoted.

The second definition is of the term 'competent authority' in each State.

Paragraph 2 of the Article provides that any term not defined in the Convention shall, unless the context otherwise requires, have the meaning which it has under the law of each State concerning the taxes to which the Convention applies.

All the conventions made by the United Kingdom contain the equivalent of para 2, along with a string of definitions which vary from one convention to another.

Paragraph 1 of Article 4 defines the term 'person domiciled in a Contracting State' as meaning any person whose estate or whose gift, under the law of that State, is liable to tax therein by reason of the domicile, residence or place of management of that person or any other criterion of a similar nature. However, the term does not include any person whose estate or whose gift is liable to tax in that State only in respect of property situated therein.

This paragraph is quite different from the 1966 Draft and is similar to the definition of 'resident of a Contracting State' in the 1977 Income Tax Model. In United Kingdom conventions made since 1975 a person is domiciled in the United Kingdom if he is domiciled there in accordance with its law or is treated as so domiciled for the purposes of a tax which is the subject of the convention. Only the Convention with the Netherlands contains a proviso (*see* p **962**) similar to the second sentence of para 1 of Article 4.

Paragraph 2 of Article 4 provides four rules for determining the status of an individual who under para 1 is domiciled in both States. Similar rules are to be found in all United Kingdom conventions except those with India and Switzerland, and they are discussed in some detail at pp **909–913**. As noted in the last paragraph on p **949**, the Convention with the United States is slightly different.

Paragraph 3 provides that where under para 1 a person other than an individual is domiciled in both States it shall be deemed to be domiciled in the State where its place of effective management is situated. This has no counterpart in United Kingdom conventions, because Capital Transfer Tax is a tax on individuals only.

Chapter III: Taxing Rules

Immovable Property

Paragraph 1 of Article 5 says that immovable property which forms part of the estate of, or of a gift made by, a person domiciled in a Contracting State and which is situated in the other Contracting State may be taxed in that other State.

The United Kingdom conventions with South Africa, the United States, the Netherlands and Sweden adopt the simpler formula of the 1966 Draft: 'Immovable property may be taxed in the Contracting State in which such property is situated.' It is not clear why the more long-winded 1982 version was thought to be advantageous. Perhaps it is intended, along with the definition in Article 3, to cater for taxes which are not strictly taxes on property: *see* the last two sentences of the first paragraph on p **929**.

Paragraph 2 defines 'immovable property' in terms similar to those of the South African and United States conventions. The proviso that debts secured by mortgage or otherwise shall not be regarded as immovable property is not in Article 5 itself but is mentioned in the Commentary as an optional addition to the Article. As noted at pp **963** and **971**, the Dutch and Swedish conventions also provide that 'immovable property' includes an interest in the proceeds of sale of land which is held on trust for sale.

Paragraph 3 says that para 1 shall also apply to immovable property of an enterprise and to immovable property used for the performance of professional services or other activities of an independent character. The conventions with South Africa, the

United States, the Netherlands and Sweden have a similar provision, which refers to 'the performance of independent personal services'. Presumably the meaning is the same.

Business Property

Under para 1 of Article 6, movable property of an enterprise which forms part of the estate of, or of a gift made by, a person domiciled in a Contracting State, which is the business property of a permanent establishment situated in the other State, may be taxed in that other State. Paragraphs 2 to 5 explain what is meant by 'permanent establishment'. Paragraph 6 extends the rule to movable property used for the performance of professional services or other activities of an independent character and pertaining to a fixed base situated in a Contracting State.

Apart from the reference to estates and gifts this Article 6 is much the same as Article 6 of the Dutch Convention (p **963**), but there is no exception for ships, boats and aircraft and no mention of partnerships. The South African and United States conventions contain additional provisions (*see* pp **931** and **952**) dealing with dependent and independent agents and associated companies: these are taken from the 1977 Income Tax Model.

Ships and Aircraft

Article 7 of the 1966 Draft contained provisions about ships, boats and aircraft similar to those of the South African, Dutch and Swedish conventions (*see* pp **932**, **963** and **971**). There is no such provision in the 1982 Model, because the Committee on Fiscal Affairs decided that Article 6 (business property) ought to apply. The United Kingdom has reserved its position on this point.

Other Property

Article 7 of the 1982 Model provides a residual rule that property, wherever situated, which forms part of the estate of, or of a gift made by, a person domiciled in a Contracting State, and not dealt with in Articles 5 and 6, is taxable only in that State.

This is similar to Article 8 of the Dutch Convention (p **964**). Article 5(1)(*a*) of the United States Convention has broadly the same effect but is subject to the exceptions in the later paragraphs of that Article (*see* pp **950–952**). Article 5(1) of the South African and Swedish conventions (pp **929** and **970**) allows the other State to tax the property if the deceased or the donor was domiciled there within the ten years immediately preceding the death or gift, and there are other exceptions more or less resembling those of the United States Convention. The Dutch Convention has a domicile-within-ten-years rule in Article 11(1) (p **965**), but it is limited to nationals of the other State.

Deduction of Debts

Article 8 of the Model lays down six rules for the deduction of debts.

1. Debts especially secured on any immovable property, or represented by the acquisition, conversion, repair or upkeep of any such property, are to be deducted from the value of that property.
2. Subject to para 1, debts pertaining to business property in Article 6 are to be deducted from the value of that property.
3. Other debts are to be deducted from the value of property in Article 7.
4. If a debt exceeds the value of the property from which it is deductible in a Contracting State under paras 1 and 2, the excess is to be deducted from the value of any other property taxable in that State.
5. Any excess still remaining in one Contracting State after the deductions in paras 3 and 4 is to be deducted from the value of the property taxable in the other State.
6. Where paras 1 to 5 would oblige one State to deduct debts to an extent greater than that provided for under its law, those paragraphs apply only to the extent that the other State is not obliged to deduct the same debts under its own law.

These rules work in two directions:

(i) they sometimes require a State to deduct debts which under its own law would not be deductible; and
(ii) they sometimes give a State the right to decline the deduction of debts which under its own law would be deductible.

If a State because of its domestic law cannot exercise its right to decline to deduct debts, Article 8 may lead to a double deduction of debts. The United Kingdom is in this uncomfortable position, because its conventions have effect only so far as they provide *relief* from Capital Transfer Tax (or for determining the *situs* of property — an outmoded concept): Finance Act 1975, Sched 7, para 7(1). Accordingly, all five of the conventions made since 1975 say merely that, in determining the amount on which tax is to be computed, permitted deductions shall be allowed under the law in force in the Contracting State in which the tax is imposed.

Article 8 does not give any definition of what is to be regarded as a deductible debt. According to the Commentary, an obligation which would not in any circumstances be regarded as a deductible debt in a Contracting State will not become deductible simply by the provisions of the Article.

Chapter IV: Methods of Eliminating Double Taxation

The Commentary explains that there are two leading principles for eliminating double taxation by the State in which the deceased or the donor was domiciled.

1. The principle of exemption, under which the State of domicile does not tax the property which under the Convention may be taxed in the other State (State of *situs*). There are two main methods:

 (*a*) The property taxable in the State of *situs* is not taken into account at all by the State of domicile. This is called 'full exemption'.

 (*b*) The property taxable in the State of *situs* is not taxed in the State of domicile, but its value is taken into account in determining the rate of tax on other property. This is called 'exemption with progression'.

2. The principle of credit, under which the State of domicile taxes the property but allows a deduction for tax paid in the State of *situs*. Here again there are two main methods:

 (*a*) The State of domicile allows all the tax paid on the property in the State of *situs*. This is called 'full credit'.

 (*b*) The deduction given by the State of domicile is restricted to that part of its own tax which is attributable to the property taxable in the State of *situs*. This is called 'ordinary credit'.

The Model Convention offers two alternative Articles, 9A giving 'exemption with progression' and 9B giving 'ordinary credit'. None of the conventions made by the United Kingdom adopts the exemption method, and so only Article 9B will be considered here. Its first paragraph says that the State of domicile shall allow as a deduction from the tax calculated according to its law an amount equal to the tax paid in the other State on any property which, in relation to the same event and in accordance with the Convention, may be taxed in that other State. The third paragraph provides that the deduction is not to exceed that part of the tax of the State of domicile which is attributable to the property in respect of which the deduction is to be allowed.

United Kingdom conventions follow these principles, but the wording of the relevant article varies widely from one convention to another. Some provisions are reciprocal, while others have separate rules for each of the two countries concerned. There are usually special provisions for settled property.

Paragraph 2 of Article 9B requires the State of domicile to allow an amount equal to the tax paid in the other State on a previous gift, to the extent that such a deduction has not been allowed under para 1 at the time of the gift. This operates in relation to tax on later gifts by the donor and on his death, where for any reason a full allowance was not made in respect of the previous gift, eg, because the tax in the State of domicile was less than in the State of *situs*. It covers cases where the domicile was unchanged and cases where the donor changed his domicile from one Contracting State to the other between the gifts or between the gift and the death. A primitive counterpart to para 2 may be found in Article 12(4)(*c*) of the South African Convention (p **935**) or Article 13(4)(*b*) of the Dutch Convention (p **967**), but the rule is limited to gifts within three years of death.

Chapter V: Special Provisions

It is not very obvious why this chapter is headed 'Special Provisions'. One might think it could equally well have been called 'General Provisions'; for there appears to be nothing special or peculiar about its five articles. Even the Irish Convention (pp **902–920**), which in most respects diverges from the Model, includes four of these articles with only slight changes of wording.

Article 10, which deals with non-discrimination, is similar to Article 24 of the 1977 Income Tax Model. It prevents discrimination against the nationals (as defined in para 2) of the other State and against stateless persons. Notwithstanding Article 2 it applies to taxes of every kind and description.

As noted at p **972**, the Swedish Convention says nothing about non-discrimination, for the good reason that the subject is already covered by the Income Tax Convention. The other post-1975 conventions all have non-discrimination articles, which are based on the Income Tax Model but relate only to capital taxes. The definition of 'national(s)' is always put into Article 3, and stateless persons are not mentioned. In the United States, where the Estate

Tax is based substantially on nationality, Article 10 does not protect a British national from being taxed as a non-resident alien.

Article 11 is concerned with the mutual agreement procedure and resembles Article 16 of the Dutch convention (*see* p **967**). It provides also that any agreement reached shall be implemented notwithstanding any time limits in the domestic laws of the Contracting States, and that the competent authorities may consult together for the elimination of double taxation in cases not provided for in the Convention.

Article 12 deals with the exchange of information and closely resembles the corresponding articles of the Irish and Dutch conventions (*see* p **920**). There is no mention of the prevention of fraud or the administration of statutory provisions against legal avoidance of tax, as there is in the conventions with South Africa, the United States and Sweden. The Article specifically provides against restriction by Article 1, so that the information may include particulars of persons not domiciled in either State.

Article 13 directs that nothing in the Convention shall affect the fiscal privileges of diplomatic agents or consular officers under the general rules of international law or under special agreements. All the conventions made by the United Kingdom since 1975 have a similar article.

Article 14 provides for extension of the Convention to any part of the territory of either State which is specifically excluded from the application of the Convention or to any State or territory for whose international relations either State is responsible, which imposes similar taxes. There are corresponding articles in the pre-1975 conventions with India, Switzerland, France and Italy, and in the post-1975 Convention with the Netherlands.

Chapter VI: Entry into Force and Termination

Under Article 15, the Convention is to enter into force when it has been ratified and the instruments of ratification have been exchanged.

Under Article 16, the Convention is to remain in force until terminated. Either State may terminate it through diplomatic channels by giving notice at least six months before the end of any calendar year after a specified year.

All the United Kingdom conventions contain articles similar to Articles 15 and 16. Those made before 1975 were to remain in force for a minimum period of three years, which is increased to five years for conventions made after 1975.

SOUTH AFRICAN DONATIONS TAX

This tax is briefly described at p **926**, where para (*b*) speaks of an exemption for gifts up to 15,000 rand made to each of the donor's children. This is not quite accurate. The exemption was for gifts to children with a limit of 15,000 rand multiplied by the number of children. The 1983 Act increases the limit to 20,000 rand with effect from 1 April 1983. Thus, if a taxpayer has four children, he may give a total of 80,000 rand tax-free to any one or more of them, less an amount equal to any previous gifts which were exempt under this provision.

The exemption ceiling for the casual gifts in para (*h*) has been increased to 5,000 rand for the year of assessment ended on or after 1 March 1983.

Meaning of 'Settlement' and Related Expressions (pp 998-1015)

The words 'for his own use or benefit' in the last line but five on p **998** presumably mean much the same as the words 'for the deceased's own use and benefit' in s 7(1) of the Finance Act 1894. This is discussed at pp **68-69**.

The decision in *Bond* v *Pickford* mentioned at pp **1008-1009** has been upheld by the Court of Appeal at [1983] STC 517. Slade LJ said that there was a crucial distinction to be drawn between (*a*) powers to alter the presently operative trusts of a settlement which expressly or by necessary implication authorise the trustees to remove assets altogether from the original settlement (without rendering any person absolutely beneficially entitled to them), and (*b*) powers of this nature which do not confer such authority on the trustees. He referred to these as 'powers in the wider form' and 'powers in the narrower form'. The first of the 'two fairly typical cases' mentioned by Lord Wilberforce in *Roome* v *Edwards* [1982] AC 279 was an example of exercising a power in the narrower form, and the second was an example of exercising a power in the wider form. The power in *Bond* v *Pickford* was indubitably in the narrower form, and its exercise did not create a new or separate settlement. Oliver LJ said that the appropriated funds remained subject to trusts which the settlement itself envisaged, and the settlement trustees remained the trustees of them with the same powers and provisions as affected the remainder of the settled funds.

Interests in Possession Generally (pp 1021–1022)

With effect from 28 January 1983 the reference to ss 3 and 4 of the Insurance Companies Act 1981 at the end of the second paragraph on p **1022** should be read as a reference to ss 3 and 4 of the Insurance Companies Act 1982.

Transfer of Interest Treated as Termination (pp 1074–1076)

In line 18 on p **1076** there should be a bracket before 'treated' as well as after 'bankrupt'.

Occupation of Property by Beneficiary Rent-free (pp 1076–1078)

The reference at the end of para (3) on p **1077** should of course be read as s 108(1)(*b*) of the Finance Act 1982.

'Surviving Spouse Exemption' (pp 1092–1116)

The citation of *A-G* v *Dodington* on p **1113** should be [1897] 2 QB 373.

Commencement of Settlement (pp 1135–1136)

Section 123 of the Finance Act 1982 was altered (perhaps rather hastily) at the report stage. The text at p **1135** inadvertently describes s 123 as it appeared in the original Bill. In fact it reads: 'Property which becomes comprised in a settlement in pursuance of a will or intestacy shall for the purposes of this Chapter be taken to have become comprised in it on the death of the testator or intestate (whether it occurred before or after the passing of this Act).'

It is not clear how this can be reconciled with s 120 of the 1982 Act in a case where a testator gives his spouse a life interest in his estate with remainder on discretionary trusts. Section 120 then treats the property as becoming comprised in a separate settlement made by the spouse when the life interest ceases, but s 123 treats it as becoming comprised in the settlement on the death of the testator.

The Ten-Yearly and Exit Charges (pp 1137–1141)

It should be noted that income in the hands of the trustees at a ten-year anniversary is subject to the ten-yearly charge. There is nothing in s 107 of the Finance Act 1982 corresponding to s 108(5), which forbids any exit charge in respect of a payment which is (or will be) income of any person for any of the purposes of income tax. Trustees can therefore save tax by distributing as much income as possible before the ten-year anniversary.

The 30 per cent grossing table in Vol 2, mentioned at p **1141**, applies only to distributions made between 9 March 1982 and 14 March 1983. For later distributions the table below may be used.

Distributions made after 14 March 1983 — grossing up at 30 per cent of full rate

Net cumulative total			*Reduced rate on slice per cent*	*Tax payable*		
£		£		£	£	£
60,000	—	79,100	4.5	Nil	+ 9/191 for each £ over	60,000
79,100	—	107,525	5.25	900	+ 21/379	79,100
107,525	—	135,725	6	2,475	+ 3/47	107,525
135,725	—	168,362.50	6.75	4,275	+ 27/373	135,725
168,362.50	—	209,987.50	7.5	6,637.50	+ 3/37	168,362.50
209,987.50	—	255,487.50	9	10,012.50	+ 9/191	209,987.50
255,487.50	—	640,337.50	10.5	14,512.50	+ 21/179	255,487.50
640,337.50	—	1,190,337.50	12	59,662.50	+ 3/22	640,337.50
1,190,337.50	—	2,336,462.50	13.5	134,662.50	+ 27/173	1,190,337.50
Over £2,336,462.50			15	313,537.50	+ 3/17	2,336,462.50

Rate of Exit Charge (pp 1150–1156)

The last paragraph on p **1152** states inaccurately that property becoming settled on a death is taken to have become comprised in the settlement immediately before the death. As noted above, s 123 of the Finance Act 1982 was amended at the report stage and provides that property settled by a will or intestacy is taken to have become comprised in the settlement on the death of the testator or intestate. However, the purpose of the section is unchanged, so that the last four lines on p **1152** and the first seven lines on p **1153** remain valid.

Property Becoming Held for Charitable or Public Purposes (pp 1156–1157)

A further example may help to illustrate the operation of s 119(3) of the Finance Act 1982. Suppose that the trustee of a discretionary trust holds 5,500 out of 10,000 shares in a private company and that a holding between 50 and 60 per cent is considered to be worth £10 a share, while one between 49 and 50 per cent is worth only £6 a share. If the trustee distributes all the shares to individual beneficiaries, tax will be payable on £55,000. The following scheme might be devised to save tax.

(1) Distribute 499 shares to individual beneficiaries. Tax is payable on £4,990.

(2) Give 2 shares to a charity. No tax is payable, apart from s 119(3).

(3) Distribute the remaining 4,999 shares to individual beneficiaries. Tax is payable on £29,994.

So, if it were not for s 119(3), only £34,984 would be taxed instead of £55,000.

In order to apply s 119(3), we must consider what tax would be charged on the gift to charity apart from s 119. The calculation would be:

	£
Value of 5,001 shares at £10	50,010
Less value of 4,999 shares at £6	29,994
	20,016

As the value of 2 shares in the hands of the charity is perhaps £2, tax is payable under s 119(3) on the excess, viz £20,014. The device is therefore useless for saving tax.

Initial Interest of Settlor or Spouse (pp 1157–1159)
Property Moving between Settlements (pp 1159–1161)

It might have been helpful to mention under these headings s 122 of the Finance Act 1982, which is discussed at pp **1139–1140**. Section 122 is designed to prevent the avoidance of tax by exploitation of ss 120 and 121. Suppose, for example, that *A*, who is domiciled outside the United Kingdom, settles foreign property on discretionary trusts for a short period with remainder to himself. *B* buys *A*'s reversion after 9 December 1981 and settles it on discretionary trusts. Under s 121 the property is treated as remaining comprised in *A*'s settlement, and apart from s 122 it would be excluded property and not liable to tax. Under s 122 it is *not* taken to be excluded property unless *B* also was domiciled outside the United Kingdom when he made his settlement.

Clause 68(1) of the Finance Bill published in March 1983 proposed to add a new subs (3) to s 121. Under this subsection s 121(1) would not apply where a reversionary interest in property expectant on the termination of a qualifying interest in possession subsisting under the first settlement was settled on the trusts of the other settlement before 10 December 1981. The intention was to remove an unintended element of retrospection from s 121. Under the previous law and practice, as explained at pp **1160-1161** and **1223**, if the reversion was settled before 10 December 1981 the property would not have been treated as remaining comprised in the first settlement.

The Chancellor of the Exchequer has announced that clause 68 will be reintroduced in 1984 and will apply to events on or after 15 March 1983. It is printed at p 58, *infra*. Where the reversion was settled before 10 December 1981 and fell into possession before 15 March 1983 the taxpayer is in no way prejudiced, because he can elect to be taxed under the old law as explained at p **1164**.

Meanings of Basic Terms (pp 1173-1188)

The Revenue are appealing against the decision of Nourse J in the *Aird (No 2)* case mentioned at pp **1172** and **1175**. It is understood that the appeal is likely to be heard towards the end of 1983.

The reference in the fifth paragraph on p **1183** to 'para 11(1)' should be to para 11(10). The reference halfway down p **1185** to 'p **660**' should be to pp **1176-1177**.

Rates of Tax: the Applicable Scales (pp 1190-1196)

The table on p **1194** applies only to distributions made between 9 March 1982 and 14 March 1983. For later distributions the table below may be used.

Distributions made after 14 March 1983 — grossing up at 20 per cent of full rate

Net cumulative total			*Reduced rate on slice per cent*	*Tax payable*			
£		£		£			£
60,000	—	79,400	3	Nil	+	3/97 for each £ over	60,000
79,400	—	108,350	3.5	600	+	7/193	79,400
108,350	—	137,150	4	1,650	+	1/24	108,350
137,150	—	170,575	4.5	2,850	+	9/191	137,150
170,575	—	213,325	5	4,425	+	1/19	170,575
213,325	—	260,325	6	6,675	+	3/47	213,325
260,325	—	660,225	7	9,675	+	7/93	260,325
660,225	—	1,235,225	8	39,775	+	2/23	660,225
1,235,225	—	2,440,975	9	89,775	+	9/91	1,235,225
Over £2,440,975			10	209,025	+	1/9	2,440,975

Survivorship Clauses (pp 1226–1233)

The decision of Nourse J in the *Aird (No 1)* case at pp **1229–1231** was unanimously reversed by the Court of Appeal at [1983] STC 700. The court agreed with the Revenue's contention that the contingency on which the interests of the settlor's two children vested was not their surviving another person by a period of one day.

There was a preliminary question which Nourse J had not thought necessary to answer. Does surviving another person by one day involve surviving for 24 hours precisely calculated from the time of the event (the 'punctum temporis' construction) or does it involve surviving for 24 hours from the end of the day on which the event occurs (the 'day excluded' construction)? After considering such cases as *Lester* v *Garland* (1808) 15 Ves 248 (cited at p 722 of the First Edition of this book) the Court held that the *prima facie* presumption was in favour of the 'day excluded' construction, and that in the *Aird* case there was nothing to displace that presumption. Considerations of convenience and certainty strongly favoured it, because it is frequently not possible to establish the precise moment of death, and where the decedent is selected by a random process his relatives may not take kindly to impertinent inquiries from complete strangers. Accordingly, what the appointment required was that Sir John Aird should survive until midnight on Sunday 30 November 1975.

Could it then be generally said that it was Sir John's surviving another person (Major Bisgood) that caused his interest to vest? Oliver LJ said it was certain that someone, somewhere, would die on Saturday 29 November. Looking at the matter on the previous day when the appointment was executed, there were the following uncertainties:

(1) Sir John might fail to survive until Monday morning, in which event the interest would fail.

(2) Sir John might survive and Monday's *Times* might carry no announcement of a death on Saturday. In that event the interest would fail. (One can ignore for the purpose of analysis the fall-back on the *Daily Telegraph*, where exactly the same considerations apply.)

(3) Sir John might survive but there might be no *Times* on Monday. In that event it would not be known whether the interest would vest or fail until the next edition was published and it could be seen whether it contained the name of a person who died on Saturday.

(4) Sir John might survive and Monday's *Times* might be published and carry the announcement of the death of a person who died on the previous Saturday. In this event the interest would vest.

In each case the vesting of the interest was contingent upon Sir John's surviving to Sunday night, but the event in each case which actually caused the interest to vest or fail would not be the death of another person on Saturday plus survival till Monday morning but the publication of *The Times*, whenever that took place. The Court therefore concluded that there was no genuine contingency of surviving another person until Monday morning within the terms of para 6(7) of Sched 5 to the Finance Act 1975. Leave to appeal to the House of Lords was refused, and it is understood that no appeal will be made.

The Newspaper-Franco device was extensively used, and no doubt in some cases the period of survival was measured in hours rather than days. It seems unlikely that that circumstance would have persuaded the Court of Appeal to a different decision. The presumption against the '*punctum temporis*' construction might be slightly less strong, but it is thought that the 'day excluded' construction would still have prevailed. Oliver LJ said that the period of one day meant and could only mean 24 hours; so he evidently made no distinction between the two terms. He added: 'One has to approach the document on the footing that it might become material to inquire whether or not the contingency expressed has occurred, and it seems to me therefore that everything points to the likelihood that those who framed the appointment would intend a meaning which was ascertainable with complete certainty and without the necessity of making any embarrassing outside inquiry'. That would apply as much to a period expressed in hours as to one expressed in days. Waller LJ said that the difficulties of adopting a construction of 24 hours from the point of time of death would be almost insuperable; and presumably he too would have held that the period of 24 hours (or any other number of hours) must run from midnight on the day of death.

The effect of the decision on other variants of the Franco device remains to be evaluated. As noted at pp **1230–1231**, the Revenue have admitted that the device gives exemption where beneficial entitlement was effectively contingent on surviving the death before 7 April 1976 of a named individual, or of the first to die of a relatively small class, such as Members of Parliament. Other variants might require the beneficiary to survive the first to die of a much larger class, such as the persons named in *Who's Who*, or might rely on selection of a decedent by a random process involving, for instance, hospitals or coroners' courts. Most of these cases have been held up to await the decision in *Aird*. In all of them the relevant question is whether survival of another person for the requisite period is genuinely the contingency upon which in the event the interest depends. As Oliver LJ said, it is no use dressing up your trusts so as to make it appear that the contingency is survival of another person when in fact it is something else.

Temporary Charitable Trusts (pp 1240–1242)

Clause 67(1) of the Finance Bill published in March 1983 proposed to insert a new subs (6A) into s 113 of the Finance Act 1982, which relates to the tapered charge of tax on property leaving a temporary charitable trust. Under the new subsection, where the tax charge is attributable wholly or partly to property which was excluded property throughout, or at any time during, the relevant period (as defined in subs (7)) no quarter throughout which that property was excluded property will be counted in calculating the rate of tax. Clause 67 was lost because of the general election, but the Chancellor of the Exchequer has announced that it will be reintroduced in 1984 and will take effect from 9 March 1982, ie, it will be retrospective to the beginning of the new discretionary trust regime. It is printed at p 58, *infra*.

The clause will apply also to the tapered charges on property leaving accumulation and maintenance trusts (p **1252**), employee trusts (p **1260**), newspaper trusts (p **1262**), protective trusts (p **1267**) and trusts for disabled persons (p **1269**).

Accumulation and Maintenance Trusts (1242–1255)

The First Condition

The decision in *Inglewood* v *IRC* [1981] STC 318 (not 91, as misprinted at p **1244**) was upheld by the Court of Appeal at [1983] STC 133. The question was whether the words 'will . . . become entitled' in para 15(1) (*a*) of Sched 5 to the Finance Act 1975 imported some degree of certainty or whether, as the trustees argued, they should be interpreted *rebus sic stantibus*, that is, unless something happens to frustrate the contingent entitlement. Vinelott J had described the trustees' construction as an impossible one. The Court of Appeal did not go as far as that, because in *Green* v *Bowes-Lyon* [1963] AC 420 the House of Lords held that in deciding whether a tenancy 'will not come to an end within 14 months or less' you must simply have regard to the question at the relevant date and not to all the future possibilities. But in *Green's* case the decision was much influenced by the context of the statute, which contained a strong indication against futurity. In *Inglewood* the context of para 15 supported the Revenue view.

The trustees argued that it did not make sense to treat 'will' as meaning 'will inevitably', because—

(*a*) a beneficiary may lawfully dispose of his interest after he attains 18 and before it vests in possession,
(*b*) his interest may be taken away from him on bankruptcy,
(*c*) his interest may be prevented from vesting in him by an order of court, eg, under the Variation of Trusts Act 1958, or
(*d*) he may die before attaining a vested interest.

The Court found no substance in point (*d*). Paragraph 15 was dealing with contingent interests. A trust could not be excluded from the operation of the paragraph because of the possible happening of an event inherent in the contingency which brought the trust within the paragraph in the first place.

The answer to points (*a*), (*b*) and (*c*) was that para 15 began with the words 'This paragraph applies to any settlement where . . .'. The Court construed 'where' as meaning 'whereby' and held that para 15 was concerned only with provisions contained in the settlement itself. None of the matters in (*a*), (*b*) and (*c*) could be so described.

More importantly the trustees contended that, if the Revenue were right, any trust which did not exclude the power of advancement in s 32 of the Trustee Act 1925 would be outside para 15. The statutory power must be exercised only for the benefit of the person contingently entitled, but the word 'benefit' has been very widely construed, so that the primary beneficiaries might be the children of that person, as in *Re Hampden* [1977] TR 177, or charities, as in *Re Clore* [1966] 1 WLR 955. The trustees argued that this power was in substance no different from a power of revocation. But the Court thought there was a vital difference: the purpose of a power of advancement is to aid the beneficial trusts and not to destroy them. It would be artificial to regard such a power as taking the trust out of para 15. The statutory power of advancement is so commonly incorporated in trusts that para 15(1)(*a*) must be read so as to accommodate it and not to withdraw the relief from a trust containing such a power.

There is to be no appeal to the House of Lords.

It may be observed that the language of s 114(1)(*a*) of the Finance Act 1982 is a little different from that of para 15(1)(*a*). 'This paragraph applies to any settlement where . . .' is replaced by 'this section applies to settled property if. . .'. It is not so easy to infer from the new wording that the conditions following the word 'if' must depend solely on the terms of the settlement. However, the official view is that s 114(1)(*a*) was not intended to change, and did not change, the law in this respect. It is thought that 'will' still imports a degree of certainty. There is much weight in the Court's conclusion that it seems 'highly unlikely that the benefit of para 15 was intended to be available to what were, in effect, discretionary trusts . . . merely by the device of a primary trust for a person at 25 which could be revoked at any time'.

THE PROTECTIVE TRUSTS TRAP

The decision of Nourse J in *Egerton* v *IRC* at [1982] STC 520 was unheld by the Court of Appeal at [1983] STC 531, [1983] TCA 450. As noted at p **1255**, the question was one of construction of s 71(2) of the Finance Act 1978, which begins by providing that the section shall be deemed to have come into force on 11 April 1978 and ends with the words 'by reason only of the coming into force of this section'. The taxpayers contended that the words quoted must refer to the actual coming into force of the section (ie, at the date of the Royal Assent) and not the deemed coming into force. The Court of Appeal rejected this construction because—

(1) The last part of s 71(2) is separated from the first part only by a semi-colon. It is not permissible to read the phrase 'the coming into force of this section' as referring to its actual coming into force, when the draftsman has provided his own dictionary by stating that the whole section shall be deemed to have come into force on another date.

(2) Section 71(2) refers to the coming into force of 'this section' rather than 'this Act', lending strength to the conclusion that it was intended to refer to something other than the coming into force of the Act itself.

(3) The words 'but' and 'only' in s 71(2) support the argument of the Crown. Reading the section (as one must)

on the footing that it came into force on 11 April 1978, one finds that the charge arises not only by reason of the coming into force of the section but by the joint effect of such coming into force and the execution of an appointment by the trustees on 19 July 1978.

(4) There is no obvious legislative purpose that would have been achieved by granting an amnesty to trusts which fell into the 'protective trusts trap' (deliberately or otherwise) between 11 April 1978 and 31 July 1978.

The taxpayers therefore failed in their attempt to join the 'club' of accumulation and maintenance trusts without paying the membership fee. There will be no appeal to the House of Lords.

Newspaper Trusts (p 1262)

The last sentence on the page appears to be wrong. The difference between the side-notes to ss 115 and 116 of the Finance Act 1982 suggests that s 115 was not intended to apply to newspaper trusts, and this may be a case where the courts would pay some attention to the side-note (*see* Lord Upjohn's remarks cited at pp 3–4, *supra*). More importantly, s 115 speaks of property 'held on trusts of the description specified in paragraph 17(1) of Schedule 5 to the Finance Act 1975', while s 116 in contrast speaks of 'property to which paragraph 17 . . . applies'. The words last cited clearly cover newspaper trusts, but the words first cited probably do not. In any case it is unlikely that a newspaper trust would satisfy all the conditions in s 115(2).

Trusts for Disabled Persons (pp 1267–1271)

The reference at p **1268** to the Mental Health Act 1959 should now be read as one to the Mental Health Act 1983.

Capital Transfer Tax Forms (pp 1273–1274)

England and Wales

The layout of Cap Form 202 has been revised and its scope extended. The new version of the form is reproduced at pp 45–48, *infra*. It is to be used where the total net value of the estate, after deducting any exemptions and reliefs claimed, does not exceed the threshold above which capital transfer tax is payable at the date of death and both

(*a*) the deceased died on or after 27 March 1981 domiciled in the United Kingdom; and (*b*) the estate comprises only property which has passed under the deceased's will or intestacy or by nomination or beneficially by survivorship; and all that property was situate in the United Kingdom.

In all other estates form 200 (UK domicile) or 201 (overseas domicile) should be used, *unless* the estate is an excepted estate under the CTT (Delivery of Account) Regulations in which case no account need be completed, although exceptionally one may be required later.

Northern Ireland

A form similar to the new English form 202 is being prepared and should soon be available.

Scotland

The Cap Form B-4 is the nearest equivalent to the form 202. Because of the new regulations (SI 1983 No 1040) mentioned at p 17, *supra*, and printed at pp 62–63, *infra*, the limit of £25,000 at p **1273** is increased to £40,000. A revised form is expected to be available early in 1984. In the meantime the present form B-4, amended where appropriate, may be used.

Inland Revenue
Capital Transfer Tax

For Official Use		
A		
Date of Grant		
Index	Reader	Stats

Inland Revenue Account

For use for an original full grant where

- **the deceased died on or after 27 March 1981 domiciled in the United Kingdom;**
- **the estate comprises only property which has passed under the deceased's Will or Intestacy or by nomination or beneficially by survivorship; and all that property was situate in the United Kingdom; and**
- **the total net value of the estate, after deducting any Exemptions and Reliefs claimed does not exceed the threshold above which Capital Transfer Tax is payable at the date of death.**

In all other cases form 200 or 201 as appropriate must be used, unless the estate is an excepted estate under the CTT (Delivery Of Accounts) Regulations. For an excepted estate no account need be completed, although exceptionally one may be required later.

Name and address of person to whom any communication should be sent ....

Reference ....

Telephone No. ....

Post town .... Postcode ....

(a) Insert "Principal" or "District" as required, and in the latter case add the name of the district.

In the High Court of Justice Family Division (Probate)

The (a) Registry

In the estate of (please use CAPITAL letters)

Surname			
Title and Forenames (*In full*)			
Date of Birth		**Date of Death**	
Last usual address		**Marital Status**	tick "✓" as appropriate married ☐ divorced ☐ single ☐ widowed ☐
		Surviving Relatives	tick "✓" as appropriate Husband ☐ Child(ren) ☐ Wife ☐ Parent(s) ☐
	Postcode	**Occupation**	

Country of Domicile (*delete as appropriate*) **England and Wales/Scotland//N Ireland**

Names and addresses of executors or intending administrators:

Postcode	**Postcode**
Postcode	**Postcode**

Cap Form 202

Declaration

(b) Insert kind of grant

No alteration is permitted to paragraphs 2, 3, 4, 5, 6 and 7.

I/We desire to obtain a grant of (b)

2. To the best of my/our knowledge and belief all the statements and particulars furnished in this account and its accompanying schedules are true and complete.

3. The deceased made no transfers of value chargeable with Capital Transfer Tax (ie no transfers of value that were not covered by the CTT exemptions) after 26 March 1974 and within 10 years of the death.

4. Account "A" is a complete and true account of all the property comprised in the estate at the death in respect of which the grant is to be made and of its value at that time.

5. Account "B" is a complete and true account of any nominated property, and of any property held jointly with any other person(s) the beneficial interest in which passed by survivorship, and of its value at the date of death.

6. No property situate outside the United Kingdom was comprised in the estate at the death.

7. The deceased did not have an interest in settled property at his death nor had he after 26 March 1974 and within 10 years of his death an interest in settled property or settled any property.

Signed by the above-named	Signed by the above-named
date	date
Signed by the above-named	Signed by the above-named
date	date

Warning: An executor or intending administrator who fails to make full enquiries and personally verify that the statements in this account are true may make himself liable to prosecution or penalties.

Account A – property of the deceased in respect of which the grant is to be made

Property without instalment option	Gross Value at date of death (before deduction of exemption(s) or relief(s))
	£
1. British Savings Bonds and other Government Securities, Savings Certificates and Premium Bonds. (Give description and state amount of each security held, attaching a schedule if necessary.) In the case of Savings Certificates please attach a letter from the Savings Certificates Division or a list giving details of purchase and value of each certificate at date of death.	
2. Other Stocks, Shares or Investments including Unit Trusts. (Give details on Form 40 or similar schedule attached and state in adjoining column total value of all investments.)	
3. Cash and Cash at Bank, Savings Banks or in Building, Co-operate or Friendly Societies, including interest to date of death (state each separately and attach a schedule if necessary).	
4. Policies of Insurance	
a. On the life of the deceased, including any bonuses thereon (state each item separately, giving names of companies).	
b. On the life of any other person (enter surrender value and attach letter from the Company).	
5. Household and Personal Goods (furniture, jewellery, clothes, car, etc).	
6. Other Assets not included above or as instalment option property opposite. (If space is insufficient please give details on schedule attached and state in adjoining column total value of these assets.)	
Total 1	

2

Debts due from the deceased	Amount
	£
1. Debts (other than mortgage and business debts)	
Name and address of creditor / Description of debt	
(If there is insufficient space to list all debts a schedule should be attached.)	
2. Funeral expenses (cost of tombstone must not be included.)	
Total 2	

Instalment option property	Gross value at date of death (before deduction of exemption(s) or relief(s))
	£
1. Freehold and leasehold property (Form 37B should also be completed) situated at ____________________ ____________________	
2. Business interests (state nature of business ____________________)	
a. Net value of deceased's interest in business, as statement or balance sheet annexed.	
b. Net value of deceased's interest as a partner in the firm of ____________________ as statement annexed.	
Total 3	

Debts due in respect of instalment option property	Amount
	£
1. Mortgages on freehold and leasehold property (amount outstanding at date of death)	
Date of mortgage ____________________	
Property on which mortgage charged ____________________ ____________________	
To whom owed ____________________	
2. Other debts (If space is insufficient please attach a schedule)	
Name and address of creditor / Description of debt	
Total 4	

Joint Property

	Tick "√" **Yes** or **No** box as appropriate
Was the deceased joint owner of any property of any description or did he hold any money on a joint account (apart from property or money of which he was merely a trustee)? If so, please give full particulars including a. the date when the joint ownership began (or the date of opening the joint account) b. the name(s) of the other owner(s) c. by whom and from what source the joint property was provided and, if it or its purchase price was contributed by one or more of the joint owners, the extent of the contribution made by each d. how the income (if any) was dealt with and enjoyed e. what is considered to be the extent of the deceased's share or interest.	**Yes** ☐ **No** ☐

Account B — Nominated and joint property	**Gross value at date of death (before deduction of exemption(s) and relief(s))**
Full description of property, real and personal, being nominated property and property held jointly with any other person(s) the beneficial interest in which passed by survivorship. (Show gross value at date of death of the proportion chargeable to tax. If space is insufficient, please attach a schedule.) Less appropriate share of debts or incumbrances thereon. (Give details. If space is insufficient, please attach a schedule.)	£
Total 5	
Value for probate purposes	£
Gross estate **per total 1**	
per total 3	
Less debts **per total 2**	
per total 4	
Net estate for probate purposes	
Value of estate for tax purposes	£
Nominated and joint property (net) — as total 5	
Net estate for Probate purposes — as above	
Deduct Exemptions and Reliefs claimed — Total 6	
1. Agricultural relief: Schedule annexed	
2. Business relief : Schedule annexed	
3. Spouse exemption: Schedule annexed	
4. Other (please specify)	
Net estate for tax purposes	

2975/5760L D8393014 100M 9/83 TP Gp 607

PART 2: STATUTES, ETC

Amendments to Vol 2

In these amendments '1975' stands for the Finance Act 1975, and so on for subsequent years.

p **25** 1975, s 26(3). The words '10(1)(*b*) or', 'given to a charity or property' and 'charity or, as the case may be, the' are repealed by F(2)A 1983, Sched 2, Pt II, with effect from 15 March 1983.

p **27** 1975, s 28(1). New subsections (1) and (1A) are substituted by F(2)A 1983, s 13(1), with effect from 26 July 1983.

p **28** 1975, s 28(8). A new subs (8) is substituted by F(2)A 1983, s 13(2), with effect from 26 July 1983.

p **35** 1975, s 37. In subs (1)(*b*) the word 'previous' is inserted before 'chargeable transfers' by 1983, Sched 9, para 3. New tables are substituted in subs (3) by F(2)A 1983, s 8(2), with effect from 15 March 1983.

pp **43-44** 1975, s 45. Subsection (1)(*c*) ceased to have effect on 15 March 1983 and has been repealed: F(2)A 1983, s 12(1) and Sched 2, Pt II. Subsections (2A) and (3) are repealed with effect from the same date.

p **48** 1975, s 51(1). The words '"charity" and "charitable" have the same meanings as in the Income Tax Acts' were omitted in error.

p **52** 1975, Sched 4, para 2. The word 'relevant' in the last line but two of subpara (2A) is changed to 'appropriate' by 1983, Sched 9, para 4.

p **55** 1975, Sched 4, para 5(3). The word 'of' at the end of line 3 of para (*b*) should be 'or'.

p **59** 1975, Sched 4, para 11(2). '£20' has become (except in Northern Ireland) level 1 on the standard scale: Criminal Justice Act 1982, ss 37, 38(1), (6) and (8), 46(1) and (4)(*a*) and 75.

p **59** 1975, Sched 4, para 12(3). The words 'a charity or only' are repealed with effect from 15 March 1983 by F(2)A 1983, Sched 2, Pt II.

pp **60-64** 1975, Sched 4, paras 13(1), 14(1) and 15. For the words 'at his option either by eight equal yearly instalments or by sixteen equal half-yearly instalments' the words 'ten equal yearly instalments' are substituted with effect from 15 March 1983 by F(2)A 1983, s 11(1). In para 13(3) '£20,000' is substituted for '£5,000' by s 11(2) with effect from the same date.

p **68** 1975, Sched 4, para 19(2). The words 'a charity or only' are repealed by F(2)A 1983, Sched 2, Pt II, with effect from 15 March 1983.

p **84** 1975, Sched 5, para 4(10). After the words 'in this paragraph' the words 'and in section 46(5)' are inserted by 1983, Sched 9, para 5.

p **101** 1975, Sched 5, para 19(4)(*a*). The date '1983' is substituted for '1959' by the Mental Health Act 1983, Sched 4, para 40.

p **111** 1975, Sched 6, para 10(1). Paragraph (*b*) has ceased to have effect in relation to transfers of value made on or after 15 March 1983 and is repealed: F(2)A 1983, s 9(1) and Sched 2, Pt II.

p **113** 1975, Sched 6, para 12. 'The Historic Buildings and Monuments Commission for England' is inserted immediately before 'The National Trust for Places of Historic Interest or Natural Beauty' by 1983, s 46(5), with effect from 13 May 1983.

p **124** 1975, Sched 7 para 1. The words 'was employed as mentioned in subpara (3) below or' and 'and not being so employed' in subpara (2) and the whole of subpara (3) where repealed by the Armed Forces Act 1981, Sched 5.

p **128** 1975, Sched 7, para 6(1). The words 'citizen of the United Kingdom and colonies' are replaced by 'British citizen, a British Dependent Territories citizen or a British Overseas citizen' with effect from 1 January 1983: British Nationality Act 1981, s 51(3).

p **163** 1975, Sched 10, para 40(4). 'Schedule 3 to the Town and Country Planning Act 1968' is replaced by 'the Compulsory Purchase (Vesting Declarations) Act 1981' under para 2 of Sched 3 to the latter Act.

p **172** 1976, s 78(4)(*b*). The words 'to the Board' and from 'or' to 'tax' are repealed by 1983, Sched 9, para 6.

pp **200–201** 1976, s 114(6). The words 'the said section 37' are replaced by 'section 37 of the said Act of 1975' by 1983, Sched 9, para 7.

p **203** 1976, s 117(5). The words 'Paragraphs 10 and 11 (gifts to charities and' are replaced by 'Paragraph 11 (gifts', and the words from 'those paragraphs' to '13 (gifts' are replaced by 'that paragraph and paragraphs 10, 12 and 13 (gifts to charities,' in relation to transfers of value made on or after 15 March 1983: F(2)A 1983, s 9(2).

p **212** 1976, Sched 10, para 2(1A). Paragraph (*b*) ceased to have effect on 15 March 1983 and has been repealed, and in para (*c*) the letters ((*bb*) have been inserted after '3(1)' with effect from that date: F(2)A 1983, s 10(1) and Sched 2, Pt II.

pp **232–233** 1977, s 49. Repealed by F(2)A 1983, Sched 2, Pt II, with effect from 15 March 1983.

p **290** 1981, Sched 14, para 2. The figure '20' in sub-paras (2) and (4) has been increased to '30' with effect from 15 March 1983 by F(2)A 1983, s 10(2), with effect from 15 March 1983.

p **304** 1982, s 92(2). Repealed by F(2)A 1983, Sched 2, Pt II, with effect from 15 March 1983.

p **311** 1982, s 103(3). The date '1981' at the foot of the page became '1982' on 28 January 1983: Insurance Companies Act 1982, Sched 5, para 28(*a*).

p **326** 1982, s 120. The word 'house' in the first line should be 'spouse'.

FINANCE ACT 1983

An Act to grant certain duties, to alter other duties and to amend the law relating to the National Debt and the Public Revenue, and to make further provision in connection with Finance.

[13 May 1983].

* * * * *

SCHEDULE 9

VALUE ADDED TAX, CAR TAX AND CAPITAL TRANSFER TAX CONSOLIDATION AMENDMENTS

* * * * *

Capital transfer tax

3 In Section 37 (1)(*b*) of the Finance Act 1975, after the words "transferred by" there shall be inserted the word "previous".

4 In paragraph 2 (2A) of Schedule 4 to that Act, for the words "relevant property" there shall be substituted the words "appropriate property".

5 In paragraph 4 (10) of Schedule 5 to that Act, after the words "in this paragraph" there shall be inserted the words "and in section 46 (5) of this Act".

6 In section 78 (4)(*b*) of the Finance Act 1976, the words "to the Board" and the words from "or" to "tax)" shall cease to have effect.

7 In section 114 (6) of that Act, for the words "the said section 37" there shall be substituted the words "section 37 of the said Act of 1975".

* * * * *

FINANCE (No 2) ACT 1983

An Act to grant certain duties, to alter other duties, and to amend the law relating to the National Debt and the Public Revenue, and to make further provision in connection with Finance.

[26 July 1983].

* * * * *

PART II

CAPITAL TRANSFER TAX

8 Reduction of tax

(1) Section 91(1) of the Finance Act 1982 (indexation of rate bands) shall not apply to chargeable transfers made in the year beginning with 6th April 1983.

(2) For the Tables in section 37(3) of the Finance Act 1975 there shall be substituted the Tables set out below.

FIRST TABLE

Portion of value		Rate of tax
Lower limit	Upper limit	Per cent
£	£	
0	60,000	Nil
60,000	80,000	30
80,000	110,000	35
110,000	140,000	40
140,000	175,000	45
175,000	220,000	50
220,000	270,000	55
270,000	700,000	60
700,000	1,325,000	65
1,325,000	2,650,000	70
2,650,000	—	75

SECOND TABLE

Portion of value		Rate of tax
Lower limit	Upper limit	Per cent
£	£	
0	60,000	Nil
60,000	80,000	15
80,000	110,000	17½
110,000	140,000	20
140,000	175,000	22½
175,000	220,000	25
220,000	270,000	30
270,000	700,000	35
700,000	1,325,000	40
1,325,000	2,650,000	45
2,650,000	—	50

(3) Subsection (2) above applies to any chargeable transfer made on or after 15th March 1983.

9 Gifts to charities

(1) In paragraph 10(1) of Schedule 6 to the Finance Act 1975 (exemption from tax for gifts to charities), paragraph (*b*) (which limits the exemption to £250,000 in respect of gifts on or within one year of the death of the transferor) shall cease to have effect.

(2) In section 117 of the Finance Act 1976 (modification of exemptions for loans) in subsection (5)—

(*a*) for the words "Paragraphs 10 and 11 (gifts to charities and" there shall be substituted the words "Paragraph 11 (gifts"; and

(*b*) for the words from "those paragraphs" to "13 (gifts" there shall be substituted the words "that paragraph and paragraphs 10, 12 and 13 (gifts to charities,".

(3) This section has effect in relation to transfers of value made on or after 15 March 1983.

10 Relief for business and agricultural property

(1) The appropriate percentage in the case of property falling within paragraph 3(1) (*bb*) of Schedule 10 to the Finance Act 1976 (relief for minority shareholdings in unquoted companies) shall be increased from 20 per cent to 30 per cent and accordingly in paragraph 2(1A) of that Schedule—

(*a*) paragraph (*b*) shall cease to have effect; and

(*b*) in paragraph (*c*), after the words "3(1)" there shall be inserted the words "(*bb*),".

(2) In sub-paragraphs (2) and (4) of paragraph 2 of Schedule 14 to the Finance Act 1981 (appropriate percentage in relation to relief for agricultural property) for the words "20 per cent" there shall, in each case, be substituted the words "30 per cent".

(3) This section has effect in relation to transfers of value made, and other events occurring, on or after 15th March 1983.

11 Payment of tax by instalments

(1) In paragraphs 13(1), 14(1) and 15 of Schedule 4 to the Finance Act 1975 (cases in which tax may be paid by instalments) for the words "at his option either by eight equal yearly instalments or by sixteen equal half-yearly instalments" there shall be subtituted the words "by ten equal yearly instalments".

(2) In paragraph 13(3) of Schedule 4 (conditions applying in relation to transfers of certain shares) for the words "£5,000" there shall be substituted the words "£20,000".

(3) This section has effect in relation to chargeable transfers made on or after 15th March 1983.

12 Domicile

(1) Section 45(1)(*c*) of the Finance Act 1975 (which treats certain persons who have become domiciled in the Channel Islands or in the Isle of Man as domiciled in the United Kingdom) shall cease to have effect.

(2) This section has effect in relation to transfers of value made, and other events occurring, on or after 15th March 1983.

13 Burden of tax

(1) In section 28 of the Finance Act 1975 (burden of tax) the following subsections shall be substituted for subsection (1)—

> "(1) Where personal representatives are liable for tax on the value transferred by a chargeable transfer made on death, the tax shall be treated as part of the general testamentary and administration expenses of the estate, but only so far as it is attributable to the value of property in the United Kingdom which—
>
> (*a*) vests in the deceased's personal representatives; and
>
> (*b*) was not, immediately before the death, comprised in a settlement.
>
> The provision made by this subsection shall have effect subject to any contrary intention shown by the deceased in his will.
>
> (1A) Where any amount of tax paid by personal representatives on the value transferred by a chargeable transfer made on death does not fall to be borne as part of the general testamentary and administration expenses of the estate, that amount shall, where occasion requires, be repaid to them by the person in whom the property to the value of which the tax is attributable is vested."

(2) For subsection (8) of that section there shall be substituted—

> "(8) References in this section (except subsection (2) to tax include references to interest on tax and, in subsections (3) to (5), to costs properly incurred in respect of tax."

(3) This section has effect where the death or other event on which tax is chargeable occurs on or after the day on which this Act is passed.

* * * * *

16 Short title, construction and repeals

(1) This Act may be cited as the Finance (No 2) Act 1983.

* * * * *

(3) Part II of this Act shall be construed as one with Part III of the Finance Act 1975.
(4) The enactments specified in Schedule 2 of this Act are hereby repealed to the extent specified in the third column of that Schedule, but subject to any provision at the end of any Part of that Schedule.

* * * * *

SCHEDULE 2

* * * * *

PART II

CAPITAL TRANSFER TAX

Chapter	Short Title	Extent of repeal
1925 c 23	The Administration of Estates Act 1925	In the First Schedule, paragraph 8 (*b*)
1955 c 24 (NI)	The Administration of Estates Act (Northern Ireland) 1955	In the First Schedule, paragraph 8 (*b*)
1975 c 7	The Finance Act 1975	In section 26(3), the words "10(1) (*b*) or", "given to a charity or property" and "charity or, as the case may be, the" In section 45, in subsection (1), paragraph (*c*) and the word "or" immediately preceding it, and subsections (2A) and (3) In Schedule 4, in paragraphs 12(3) and 19(2), the words "a charity or only" In Schedule 6, in paragraph 10(1), paragraph (*b*) and the word "and" immediately preceding it
1976 c 40	The Finance Act 1976	In Schedule 10, paragraph 2 (1A) (*b*)
1977 c 36	The Finance Act 1977	Section 49
1982 c 39	The Finance Act 1982	Section 92 (2)

1 The repeals in the Administration of Estates Act 1925 and the Administration of Estates Act (Northern Ireland) 1955 have effect in relation to deaths on or after the day on which this Act was passed.

2 The repeals of—

(*a*) subsections (1)(*c*), (2A) and (3) of section 45 of the Finance Act 1975,

(*b*) paragraph 2 (1A) (*b*) of Schedule 10 to the Finance Act 1976, and

(*c*) section 49 of the Finance Act 1977,

have effect in relation to transfers of value made, and other events occurring, on or after 15th March 1983.

3 The remaining repeals have effect in relation to transfers of value made on or after 15th March 1983.

FINANCE BILL, MARCH 1983

Note The following four clauses were not enacted in 1983 but are to be re-introduced as part of the Finance Bill 1984. The commencement dates of the four provisions, however, will be as follows:

67	9 March 1982
68	15 March 1983
71	1 April 1983
72	Date of Royal Assent to Finance Act 1984

67 Special discretionary trusts: excluded property

(1) In section 113 of the Finance Act 1982 (charge to tax in respect of property leaving temporary charitable trusts) the following subsection shall be inserted after subsection (6) and will accordingly be applied by sections 114 (accumulation and maintenance trusts), 116 (property leaving employee trusts and newspaper trusts) and 118 (protective trusts and trusts for disabled persons) of that Act—

> "(6A) Where the whole or part of the amount on which tax is charged under this section is attributable to property which was excluded property throughout, or at any time during, the relevant period then, in determining the rate at which tax is charged under this section in respect of that amount or part, no quarter throughout which that property was excluded property shall be counted.".

(2) In subsection (7) of section 113 which defines "relevant period" for the purposes of subsection (6), for the words "subsection (6)" there shall be substituted the words "subsections (6) and (6A)".

(3) This section has effect in relation to events on or after 9th March 1982.

68 Property moving between settlements

(1) In section 121 of the Finance Act 1982 (property moving between settlements), the following subsection shall be added at the end—

> "(3) Subsection (1) above does not apply where a reversionary interest in the property expectant on the termination of a qualifying interest in possession subsisting

under the first settlement was settled on the trusts of the other settlement before 10th December 1981.".

(2) In paragraph 3 of Schedule 7 to the Finance Act 1975 (certain government securities to be excluded property if person beneficially entitled is domiciled and ordinarily resident abroad) the following sub-paragraph shall be inserted after sub-paragraph (2A)—

"(2AA). Sub-paragraph (2A) above does not apply where a reversionary interest in the property expectant on the termination of a qualifying interest in possession subsisting under the first settlement was settled on the trusts of the second settlement before 10th December 1981.".

(3) This section has effect in relation to events on or after 15th March 1983.

71 Adjustment of tax

(1) In paragraph 23(3) of Schedule 4 to the Finance Act 1975 (adjustment of tax in cases of fraud, wilful default or neglect), for the words "a person liable for the tax, the period" there shall be substituted the words "any of the following—

(*a*) a person liable for the tax; and

(*b*) in the case of tax chargeable under Chapter II of Part IV of the Finance Act 1982, the person who is the settlor in relation to the settlement;

the period".

(2) With effect from 1st April 1983, subsection (8) of section 114 of the Finance Act 1976 (transfers reported late) shall cease to have effect.

(3) Sub-paragraph (1) above has effect in relation to any fraud, wilful default or neglect coming to the knowledge of the Commissioners of Inland Revenue on or after 1st April 1983.

72 Recovery of tax

In Schedule 4 to the Finance Act 1975, after paragraph 22 there shall be inserted—

"22A. In Scotland, tax and interest on tax may, without prejudice to any other remedy, and if the amount of the tax and interest does not exceed the sum for the time being specified in section 35(1)(*a*) of the Sheriff Courts (Scotland) Act 1971, be sued for and recovered in the sheriff court.

22B. An officer of the Board who is authorised by the Board to do so may address the court in any proceedings in a county court or sheriff court for the recovery of tax or interest on tax."

The Estate Duty (Interest on Unpaid Duty) Order 1982 (SI 1982 No 1584)

The Treasury, in exercise of the powers conferred on them by section 30 of the Finance Act 1970, hereby make the following Order:—

1 This order may be cited as the Estate Duty (Interest on Unpaid Duty) Order 1982 and shall come into operation on 1st December 1982.

2 The rate of interest payable under the following enactments, namely—

(*a*) section 18 of the Finance Act 1896;

(*b*) section 61(5) of the Finance (1909-10) Act 1910 as amended by section 9 of the Finance Act 1912; and

(*c*) section 17(3) of the Law of Property Act 1925 and section 73(6) of the Land Registration Act 1925.

shall, as regards interest accruing on or after 1st December 1982, be 6 per cent. instead of 9 per cent., per annum.

3 Section 8(9) of the Finance Act 1894 shall, as regards interest accruing on or after 1st December 1982, have effect with the substitution of the word "six" for the word "nine".

The Capital Transfer Tax (Interest on Unpaid Tax) Order 1982 (SI 1982 No 1585)

The Treasury, in exercise of the powers conferred on them by paragraph 19 of Schedule 4 to the Finance Act 1975, hereby make the following Order:—

1 This Order may be cited as the Capital Transfer Tax (Interest on Unpaid Tax) Order 1982 and shall come into operation on 1st December 1982.

2 The prescribed rate of interest on any unpaid tax on which interest is payable under paragraph 19(1) of Schedule 4 to the Finance Act 1975 shall be:

(*a*) if the chargeable transfer was made on death, 6 per cent., instead of 9 per cent., per annum

(*b*) in any other case, 8 per cent., instead of 12 per cent., per annum.

The Capital Transfer Tax (Delivery of Accounts) (No 3) Regulations 1983 (SI 1983 No 1039)

The Commissioners of Inland Revenue, in exercise of the powers conferred on them by section 94(1) of the Finance Act 1980, hereby make the following Regulations:

Citation, commencement and extent

1 These Regulations may be cited as the Capital Transfer Tax (Delivery of Accounts (No 3) Regulations 1983 and shall come into operation on 1st September 1983.

2 These Regulations do not extend to Scotland or Northern Ireland.

Interpretation

3 In these Regulations "the Principal Regulations" means The Capital Transfer Tax (Delivery of Accounts) Regulations 1981.

Amendments to Principal Regulations

4 In Regulation 3 of the Principal Regulations

(*a*) in paragraph (*b*) for "£25,000" there shall be substituted "£40,000";

(*b*) in paragraph (*c*) for "£1,000" there shall be substituted "£2,000";

(*c*) in paragraph (*d*) for "1st April 1981" there shall be substituted "1st April 1983".

The Capital Transfer Tax (Delivery of Accounts) (Scotland) (No 2) Regulations 1983 (SI 1983 No 1040)

The Commissioners of Inland Revenue, in exercise of the powers conferred on them by section 94(1) of the Finance Act 1980, hereby make the following Regulations:

Citation, commencement and extent

1 These Regulations may be cited as the Capital Transfer Tax (Delivery of Accounts) (Scotland) (No 2) Regulations 1983 and shall come into operation on 1 September 1983.

2 These Regulations extend to Scotland only.

Interpretation

3 In these Regulations 'the Principal Regulations' means The Capital Transfer Tax (Delivery of Accounts) (Scotland) Regulations 1981.

(DELIVERY OF ACCOUNTS) (SCOTLAND) REGULATIONS 63

Amendments to Principal Regulations

4 In Regulation 3 of the Principal Regulations

(*a*) in paragraph (*b*) for '£25,000' there shall be substituted '£40,000';

(*b*) in paragraph (*c*) for '£1,000' there shall be substituted '£2,000';

(*c*) in paragraph (*d*) for '1st April 1981' there shall be substituted '1st April 1983'.

The OECD Model Double Taxation Convention on Estates and Inheritances and on Gifts (1982)

SUMMARY OF THE CONVENTION

TITLE OF THE CONVENTION

Convention between (State A) and (State B) for the avoidance of double taxation with respect to taxes on estates and inheritances and on gifts.

PREAMBLE OF THE CONVENTION

Note: The Preamble of the Convention shall be drafted in accordance with the constitutional procedure of both Contracting States.

Chapter I

SCOPE OF THE CONVENTION

1 Estates, inheritances and gifts covered

This Convention shall apply:

(*a*) to estates and inheritances where the deceased was domiciled, at the time of his death, in one or both of the Contracting States, and

(*b*) to gifts where the donor was domiciled, at the time of the gift, in one or both of the Contracting States.

2 Taxes covered

(1) This Convention shall apply to taxes on estates and inheritances and on gifts imposed on behalf of a Contracting State or of its political subdivisions or local authorities, irrespective of the manner in which they are levied.

(2) There shall be regarded as taxes on estates and inheritances taxes imposed by reason of death in the form of taxes on the *corpus* of the estate, of taxes on inheritances, of transfer duties, or of taxes on *donationes mortis causa*. There shall be regarded as taxes on gifts taxes imposed on transfers *inter vivos* only because such transfers are made for no, or less than full, consideration.

(3) The existing taxes to which the Convention shall apply are:

(*a*) (in State A) ....

(*b*) (In State B) ....

(4) The Convention shall apply also to any identical or substantially similar taxes which are imposed after the date of signature of the Convention in addition to, or in place of, the existing taxes. At the end of each year, the competent authorities of the Contracting States shall notify each other of changes which have been made in their respective taxation laws.

Chapter II

DEFINITIONS

3 General definitions

(1) For the purposes of this Convention, unless the context otherwise requires:

(*a*) the term "property which forms part of the estate of, or of a gift made by, a person domiciled in a Contracting State" includes any property the devolution or transfer of which, under the law of a Contracting State, is liable to a tax covered by the Convention;

(*b*) the term "competent authority" means;

(i) (in State A) ....

(ii) (in State B) ....

(2) As regards the application of the Convention by a Contracting State, any term not defined therein shall, unless the context otherwise requires, have the meaning which it has under the law of that State concerning the taxes to which the Convention applies.

4 Fiscal domicile

(1) For the purposes of this Convention, the term "person domiciled in a Contracting State" means any person whose estate or whose gift, under the law of that State, is liable to tax therein by reason of the domicile, residence or place of management of that person or any other criterion of a similar nature. However, this term does not include any person whose estate or whose gift is liable to tax in that State only in respect of property situated therein.

(2) Where by reason of the provisions of paragraph (1) an individual is domiciled in both Contracting States, then his status shall be determined as follows:

(*a*) he shall be deemed to be domiciled in the State in which he has a permanent home available to him; if he has a permanent home available to him in both States, he shall be deemed to be domiciled in the State with which his personal and economic relations are closer (centre of vital interests);

(*b*) if the State in which he has his centre of vital interests cannot be determined, or if he has not a permanent home available to him in either State, he shall be deemed to be domiciled in the State in which he has an habitual abode;

(*c*) if he has an habitual abode in both States or in neither of them, he shall be deemed to be domiciled in the State of which he is a national;

(*d*) if he is a national of both States or of neither of them, the competent authorities of the Contracting States shall settle the question by mutual agreement.

(3) Where by reason of the provisions of paragraph (1) a person other than an individual is domiciled in both Contracting States, then it shall be deemed to be domiciled in the State in which its place of effective management is situated.

Chapter III

TAXING RULES

5 Immovable property

(1) Immovable property which forms part of the estate of, or of a gift made by, a person domiciled in a Contracting State and which is situated in the other Contracting State may be taxed in that other State.

(2) The term "immovable property" shall have the meaning which it has under the law of the Contracting State in which the property in question is situated. The term shall in any case include property accessory to immovable property, livestock and equipment used in agriculture and forestry, rights to which the provisions of general law respecting landed property apply, usufruct of immovable property and rights to variable or fixed payments as consideration for the working of, or the right to work, mineral deposits, sources and other natural resources; ships, boats and aircraft shall not be regarded as immovable property.

(3) The provisions of paragraph (1) shall also apply to immovable property of an enterprise and to immovable property used for the performance of professional services or other activities of an independent character.

6 Movable property of a permanent establishment or a fixed base

(1) Movable property of an enterprise which forms part of the estate of, or of a gift made by, a person domiciled in a Contracting State, which is the business property of a permanent establishment situated in the other Contracting State, may be taxed in that other State.

(2) For the purposes of this Convention, the term "permanent establishment" means a fixed place of business through which the business of an enterprise is wholly or partly carried on.

(3) The term "permanent establishment" includes especially:

(*a*) a place of management;

(*b*) a branch;
(*c*) an office;
(*d*) a factory;
(*e*) a workshop; and
(*f*) a mine, an oil or gas well, a quarry or any other place of extraction of natural resources.

(4) A building site or construction or installation project constitutes a permanent establishment only if it lasts more than twelve months.

(5) Notwithstanding the preceding provisions of this Article, the term "permanent establishment" shall be deemed not to include:

(*a*) the use of facilities solely for the purpose of storage, display or delivery of goods or merchandise belonging to the enterprise;
(*b*) the maintenance of a stock of goods or merchandise belonging to the enterprise solely for the purpose of storage, display or delivery;
(*c*) the maintenance of a stock of goods or merchandise belonging to the enterprise solely for the purpose of processing by another enterprise;
(*d*) the maintenance of a fixed place of business solely for the purpose of purchasing goods or merchandise, or of collecting information, for the enterprise;
(*e*) the maintenance of a fixed place of business solely for the purpose of carrying on for the enterprise any other activity of a preparatory or auxiliary character; or
(*f*) the maintenance of a fixed place of business solely for any combination of activities mentioned in subparagraphs (*a*) to (*e*), provided that the overall activity of the fixed place of business resulting from this combination is of a preparatory or auxiliary character.

(6) Movable property which forms part of the estate of, or of a gift made by, a person domiciled in a Contracting State, used for the performance of professional services or other activities of an independent character and pertaining to a fixed base situated in the other Contracting State, may be taxed in that other State.

7 Other property

Property, wherever situated, which forms part of the estate of, or of a gift made by, a person domiciled in a Contracting State, and not dealt with in Articles 5 and 6, shall be taxable only in that State.

8 Deduction of debts

(1) Debts especially secured on any property referred to in Article 5 shall be deducted from the value of that property. Debts, not being especially secured on any property referred to in Article 5, which are represented by the acquisition, conversion, repair or upkeep of any such property, shall be deducted from the value of that property.
(2) Subject to the provisions of paragraph (1), debts pertaining to a permanent establishment referred to in paragraph (1) of Article 6, or to a fixed base referred to in paragraph (6) of Article 6, shall be deducted from the value of the permanent establishment or the fixed base as the case may be.
(3) Other debts shall be deducted from the value of property to which the provisions of Article 7 apply.
(4) If a debt exceeds the value of the property from which it is deductible in a Contracting State, according to the provisions of paragraphs (1) or (2), the excess shall be deducted from the value of any other property taxable in that State.
(5) Any excess still remaining in one Contracting State after the deductions referred to in paragraphs (3) or (4) shall be deducted from the value of the property liable to tax in the other Contracting State.
(6) Where the provisions of paragraphs (1) to (5) would oblige one Contracting State to deduct debts to an extent greater than that provided for under its law, those provisions shall apply only to the extent that the other Contracting State is not obliged to deduct the same debts under its own law.

Chapter IV

METHODS FOR ELIMINATING DOUBLE TAXATION

9A Exemption method

(1) The Contracting State in which the deceased was domiciled at his death, or the donor was domiciled at the time of the gift, shall exempt from tax any property which, in relation to the same event and in accordance with the provisions of this Convention, may be taxed in the other Contracting State.
(2) The former Contracting State shall also exempt from tax any property which, in relation to a previous gift and in accordance with the provisions of the Convention, may have been taxed in the

other Contracting State. That former State, however, shall not exempt from tax any property which was taxable in that State in accordance with the provisions of Articles 5 or 6 of the Convention.
(3) In each case the former Contracting State may take the exempted property into account in calculating the amount of tax on any remaining property.

9B Credit method

(1) The Contracting State in which the deceased was domiciled at his death, or the donor was domiciled at the time of the gift, shall allow as a deduction from the tax calculated according to its law an amount equal to the tax paid in the other Contracting State on any property which, in relation to the same event and in accordance with the provisions of this Convention, may be taxed in that other State.
(2) The former Contracting State shall also allow as a deduction from such tax an amount equal to the tax which has been paid in the other Contracting State on a previous gift in accordance with the provisions of the Convention to the extent that such a deduction has not been allowed under the provisions of paragraph (1) at the time of that gift. That former State, however, shall not allow a deduction in respect of tax paid on property which was taxable in that State in accordance with the provisions of Articles 5 or 6 of the Convention.
(3) The deductions referred to in paragraphs (1) and (2) shall not, however, exceed that part of the tax of the former Contracting State, as computed before any deduction is made, which is attributable to the property in respect of which the deduction is to be allowed.

Chapter V

SPECIAL PROVISIONS

10 Non-discrimination

(1) Nationals of a Contracting State, wherever they are domiciled, shall not be subjected in the other Contracting State to any taxation, or any requirement connected therewith, which is other or more burdensome than the taxation and connected

requirements to which nationals of that other State in the same circumstances are or may be subjected.

(2) The term "nationals" means:

(*a*) all individuals possessing the nationality of a Contracting State;

(*b*) all legal persons, partnerships and associations deriving their status as such from the law in force in a Contracting State.

(3) Stateless persons who are domiciled in a Contracting State shall not be subjected in either Contracting State to any taxation, or any requirement connected therewith, which is other or more burdensome than the taxation and connected requirements to which nationals of the State concerned in the same circumstances are or may be subjected.

(4) The provisions of this Article shall, notwithstanding the provisions of Article 2, apply to taxes of every kind and description.

11 Mutual agreement procedure

(1) Where a person considers that the actions of one or both of the Contracting States result or will result for him in taxation not in accordance with the provisions of this Convention, he may, irrespective of the remedies provided by the domestic laws of those States, present his case to the competent authority of either Contracting State. The case must be presented within three years from the first notification of the action resulting in taxation not in accordance with the provisions of the Convention.

(2) The competent authority, if the objection appears to it to be justified and if it is not itself able to arrive at a satisfactory solution, shall endeavour to resolve the case by mutual agreement with the competent authority of the other Contracting State, with a view to the avoidance of taxation which is not in accordance with the provisions of the Convention. Any agreement reached shall be implemented notwithstanding any time limits in the domestic laws of the Contracting States.

(3) The competent authorities of the Contracting States shall endeavour to resolve by mutual agreement any difficulties or doubts arising as to the interpretation or application of the Convention. They may also consult together for the elimination of double taxation in cases not provided for in the Convention.

(4) The competent authorities of the Contracting States may communicate with each other directly for the purpose of reaching an agreement in the sense of the preceding paragraphs. When it

seems advisable in order to reach agreement to have an oral exchange of opinions, such exchange may take place through a Commission consisting of representatives of the competent authorities of the Contracting States.

12 Exchange of information

(1) The competent authorities of the Contracting States shall exchange such information as is necessary for carrying out the provisions of this Convention or of the domestic laws of the Contracting States concerning taxes covered by the Convention insofar as the taxation thereunder is not contrary to the Convention. The exchange of information is not restricted by Article 1. Any information received by a Contracting State shall be treated as secret in the same manner as information obtained under the domestic laws of that State and shall be disclosed only to persons or authorities (including courts and administrative bodies) involved in the assessment or collection of, the enforcement or prosecution in respect of, or the determination of appeals in relation to, the taxes covered by the Convention. Such persons or authorities shall use the information only for such purposes. They may disclose the information in public court proceedings or in judicial decisions.

(2) In no case shall the provisions of paragraph (1) be construed so as to impose on a Contracting State the obligation:

- (*a*) to carry out administrative measures at variance with the laws or administrative practice of that or of the other State;
- (*b*) to supply information which is not obtainable under the laws, or in the normal course of the administration, of that or of the other State;
- (*c*) to supply information which would disclose any trade, business, industrial, commercial or professional secret or trade process, or information, the disclosure of which would be contrary to public policy (ordre public).

13 Diplomatic agents and consular officers

Nothing in this Convention shall affect the fiscal privileges of diplomatic agents or consular officers under the general rules of international law or under the provisions of special agreements.

14 Territorial extension

(1) This Convention may be extended, either in its entirety or with any necessary modifications, [to any part of the territory of (State A) or of (State B) which is specifically excluded from the application of the Convention or] to any State or territory for whose international relations (State A) or (State B) is responsible, which imposes taxes substantially similar in character to those to which the Convention applies. Any such extension shall take effect from such date and subject to such modifications and conditions, including conditions as to termination, as may be specified and agreed between the Contracting States in notes to be exchanged through diplomatic channels or in any other manner in accordance with their constitutional procedures.
(2) Unless otherwise agreed by both Contracting States, the termination of the Convention by one of them under Article 16 shall also terminate, in the manner provided for in that Article, the application of the Convention [to any part of the territory of (State A) or of (State B) or] to any State or territory to which it has been extended under this Article.

Note: The words between square brackets are of relevance when, by special provision, a part of the territory of a Contracting State is excluded from the application of the Convention.

Chapter VI

FINAL PROVISIONS

15 Entry into force

(1) This Convention shall be ratified and the instruments of ratification shall be exchanged at .... as soon as possible.
(2) The Convention shall enter into force upon the exchange of instruments of ratification and its provisions shall have effect:

(*a*) (in State A) ....

(*b*) (in State B) ....

16 Termination

This Convention shall remain in force until terminated by a Contracting State. Either Contracting State may terminate the Convention, through diplomatic channels, by giving notice of termination at least six months before the end of any calendar year after the year .... In such event, the Convention shall cease to have effect:

(*a*) (in State A) ....

(*b*) (in State B) ....

TERMINAL CLAUSE

Note: The terminal clause shall be drafted in accordance with the constitutional procedure of both Contracting States.

INDEX